TABLE OF CONTENTS

CHAPTER ONE

THE WORD OF GOD

A Fool or a Doer

When I was a teenager, our church had a Bible reading program. Sunday School teachers would ask the students to raise their hands if they'd read their Bible every day that week. It was an ongoing crisis in my life.

Lying about reading my Bible had to be about the most wrong thing I could do. Surely in the (imaginary!) ranking of sins, it must be at least doubly bad! But remembering to read my Bible (or for that matter remembering if I had read my Bible) was tough. Many nights I was half-asleep with the lights out, when suddenly I'd sit bolt upright in bed. I'd pad over to the light switch in my pajamas, pull my Bible off the book shelf, and read a verse or two from the Psalms or a four- or five-verse story from the Gospels. Then I'd crawl back into my bed satisfied.

The elders certainly did not intend to cause crises of conscience in high schoolers throughout the congregation when they decided to implement that program. And I'd like to say that I would never do something similar as an adult.

But that would be a lie, and we've already talked about that.

I, like I suspect the rest of us, have a long-established mental check list. Near the top, just below "Go to church" and just above "Pray," is "Read my Bible." If we forget, we feel guilty, but if we can just slam in five verses from Psalms, we mark it off with a huff of secret relief.

Why secret? Because we know it's wrong.

We know we are supposed to long for the milk of the Word (1 Peter 2:1-3). We know that somewhere out there are super Christians who read for hours a day, who know their Scriptures like we know the songs on the radio, and who get something out of what they read. But hey, at least we're reading, right? We get credit, too! Don't we?

No.

Hidden at the end of the Sermon on the Mount is the story of the two foundations. Most of us only know it from the song, "The Wise Man Built His House upon the Rock."

The song, while catchy, has the idea slightly wrong. The first two verses, "The wise man built his house upon the rock" and "The foolish man built his house upon the sand" are entirely unobjectionable. The last verse however says this: "So build your life on the Lord Jesus Christ and the blessings will come down." There's nothing with which to disagree in the sentiment; it is just not what the verses actually say.

> Therefore everyone who hears these words of Mine and acts on them, may be compared to a wise man who built his house on the rock. And the rain fell, and the floods came, and the winds blew and slammed against that house; and yet it did not fall, for it had been founded on the rock. Everyone who hears these words of Mine and does not act on them, will be like a foolish man who built his house on the sand. The rain fell, and the floods came, and the winds blew and slammed against that house; and it fell—and great was its fall (Matthew 7:24-27).

When I hopped up out of bed, skimmed a few verses, and slid smugly back between the covers, I was a fool. I heard the Word, but I was not reading to obey. I wasn't acting on the Word of God. I don't mean as a young teen I was actively rebelling against God, not at all. But when I read, "If possible, so far as it depends on you, be at peace with all men" (Romans 12:18), it didn't even dawn on me that I should exasperate my sister less. And when I read that God hates pride, I never connected it to my own teenage arrogance (Proverbs 8:13). I heard the Word of God, but I did not act on it, and Jesus says I was a foolish person whose house was in for a crash.

Individual Questions

1. How many days a week do you actually read your Bible? How many minutes each time?

   Growing up, We did Not have a Bible

2. Think of an instance where you read the Word of God but didn't act on it.

Group Questions

. . . .

1. What kind of "great fall" might happen to a person who heard but did not act on Jesus' words?

_____

_____

_____

2. The Sermon on the Mount (Matthew 5-7) is the immediate context of Jesus' story of the two foundations. What words in this sermon are often heard (or quoted) but rarely acted upon?

_____

_____

_____

So if three verses quickly read and quickly forgotten do us no good, should we just give up reading? If all I have is five minutes (and any mother of a newborn knows that sometimes you literally only have five minutes), should I just not bother? Do I need a quiet hour on my porch before the day begins? Perhaps I need highlighters, dictionaries, commentaries, and concordances? No, as nice as those might be, they are not the key.

As a certifiable nerd I tended to think that sheer knowledge could turn the lock. While a student at Harding University, I had a chance to gain insight into the original language, background, and context of the writers of the Bible. Although it certainly helped my Bible study, I was surprised to discover that many of the scholars I was reading, leaders in the field of Bible research, were themselves unbelievers. Neither time in the Word nor scholarship made them wise men who acted on the Word of God. Time and scholarship won't necessarily help us either.

Somehow, we have to find a way to read the Bible in a new way. No matter how helpful, we don't need scholarship to obey the Word. We don't even need to neglect our work, our children, our husbands, or the laundry to begin to obey the Word. No. What we need is a new way of reading—a way tuned to putting into immediate action what we read.

The Brat, the Liar, and the Idiot

Jesus is not the only person in the Bible who had harsh words for those who have access to the Word of God but walk away unchanged. James has an ironically well-known statement about this, too. It's ironic because we often hear but rarely apply James' words about being doers rather than hearers of the Word.

James begins by instructing his readers to put away all that was filthy from their former lives and instead "in humility receive the Word implanted" (James 1:21). This dense phrase deserves further attention. The receiver has little active part in getting a gift. The soil has even less part as seeds are implanted in it. These words, *implant* and *receive* emphasize that God is active. His Word, His self-revelation is itself a gift to be received. Like a farmer or a vine grower from the parable, He scatters His Word into the hearts of men. So do we have any part in the phrase "in humility receive the Word implanted?" Yes, humility, which is also called meekness.

Meekness is not a concept we like. It seems to run counter-cultural to American values like individualism, pluck, self-esteem, and pride. But what if we applied a little imagination? What would a meek child be like? She wouldn't argue, sulk, or fuss. There wouldn't be any glares, delays, or slammed doors. Our advice would be taken with the utmost seriousness; this child would trust our words because we had her best interests at heart. The only thing limiting such a child would be her parent's wisdom. Every mama longs for a meek child.

And if our child wasn't meek? When we refused her some privilege or treat, she would be sure that we just didn't want her to have any fun. She wouldn't trust us to order her life. She'd roll those eyes and explain all the reasons she couldn't obey. The reason we look back now and sigh, "If only I knew then, what I know now" is because we refused to hear our parent's words meekly.

We are children of God. James insists that we must not be the brat who is convinced that God is trying to take all the fun out of life. Generously, God gives the Word; we receive it. He implants the Word; we open ourselves to it. We have the wisest heavenly Father; we need only meekly accept what He offers.

But if we refuse to meekly receive? If we are merely hearers and not a doers, what could happen?

Self-deception.

But prove yourselves doers of the word, and not merely hearers who delude themselves (James 1:22).

James diagnoses the "hearers'" problem. They are fooling themselves. To borrow another example from our children, can you imagine a child who smiles and agrees with you that loving one another is crucial and then insults her sister? Or a son who talks with the younger kids about how important it is to stand up for their faith, but his walk with Christ is non-existent at school? Although we might brand them hypocrites, I suspect it is just as likely that they are self-deluded. It is quite possible for us, too, to hear the Word on Sunday morning, nod our collective heads, and believe that since we agree with God, we're all good. Intellectual agreement, however, with no action is the same as lying to ourselves.

Jeremiah's words ring true, "The heart is more deceitful than all else and is desperately sick; Who can understand it? I, the LORD, search the heart, I test the mind, Even to give to each man according to his ways, According to the results of his deeds" (Jeremiah 17: 9-10). God knows our hearts. He tests our minds. And if our hearts have been deceiving us, if we've been nodding agreement while letting the words slide off of us like water off a duck's back, God knows. He will judge us accordingly.

We've thought about the way we could be brats: delaying, excusing, and ignoring. We've talked about how we could be liars, refusing to search our hearts and see the truth about ourselves. But James has one more painful comment.

For if anyone is a hearer of the word and not a doer, he is like a man who looks at his natural face in a mirror; for *once* he has looked at himself and gone away, he has immediately forgotten what kind of person he was. But one who looks intently at the perfect law, the *law* of liberty, and abides by it, not having become a forgetful hearer but an effectual doer, this man will be blessed in what he does (James 1:23-25).

James says the person who hears but doesn't act is like a social idiot who can't remember what she looks like long enough to fix her own hair or get the spinach out of her teeth. Jesus calls the man who hears but doesn't act a fool. It's not enough to hear the Word. God does not want us to be "hearers" but meek, honest, and transformable "doers," constantly receiving correction from God's Word and implementing it in our lives.

Individual Questions

1. Are you more likely to be The Brat (without meekness), The Liar (self-deceived), or The Idiot (forgetting to change)? Think of a personal example of each problem. For example, "I act like the idiot when I agree on Sunday that gossiping is wrong and then on Monday I stand around the break room just waiting to share a piece of news I heard."

   A. The Brat _____

   _____

   _____

B. The Liar _____

_____

_____

C. The Idiot _____

_____

_____

2. How does the admonition "Just follow your heart" line up with Jeremiah's words (Jeremiah 17:9-10)?

_____

_____

_____

Group Questions
. . . .

1. How can we help one another overcome these three attitudes? Or in more positive terms, how do we develop meekness, painful self-reflection, and a desire to change in ourselves, our sisters, and the young people in our lives?

_____

_____

_____

_____

2. What would it look like if a person looked intently into the "law of liberty"? What kind of self-examination is implied by James in this passage?

_____

_____

_____

Reading Better

If we have determined not to be fools but to set our minds to hear and do what God said, then it is time for us to think about reading our Bibles better. Not simply more often, though for some of us that would be a positive step. And not even with more background, language study, or scholarly opinion. Although for some that might be helpful, for others it would simply be a distraction—an intellectual barrier between them and meekly receiving the Word.

I hope instead that we can learn to read with the right attitudes of heart. A well-known example will serve to illustrate what is hampering us. Let's turn our attention to the "Excellent Wife."

She's been the target of women's aggravation for centuries. You may have run across her in a ladies' Bible study book or a sermon. Or perhaps you simply read her description one day and were amazed by the poetic description (Proverbs 31:10-31). Were you able to hear the verses, gaze intently into your own marriage or household, and change? What stopped you? Let's take one verse for an example.

She rises also while it is still night and gives food to her household and portions to her maidens (Proverbs 31:15).

When you just read this, how did you feel? Irritated? Angry? Did you feel attacked?

"Well, I can't get up before dawn every morning! No one at my house eats breakfast! Why should all the burden be on me anyway? Why can't somebody else get up and deal with the food? I am already overworked and under-appreciated!"

Or perhaps, as you read, you lacked the imagination to see how this could play out in your life.

What am I supposed to do? I don't have maidens or other servants to help me, and I don't live in some ancient "household," just a single-wide trailer. I don't make dinner before dawn. This has nothing to do with me and my situation.

Worst of all did you feel that the words were impractical, idealistic, something no one could possibly obey? Did you read them radically?

This Proverbs 31 woman is just poetry. No one I knows gets up before dawn to do anything. She must have been like June Cleaver: perfect house, perfect husband, delightfully naughty children managed without a hair or opinion out of place. No. That could never be me and my family. It's just an impossible ideal.

Let's try reversing the process. A little imagination will give us new insight. Here's a creative paraphrase of the verse.

She sets her alarm before daybreak,

making breakfast for her husband

and packing lunches for her kids.

How about our irritable and defensive reading? Does the verse demand we always rise early or that no one help us? No. It does seem though that this woman, an example of an excellent wife, wasn't afraid of getting up early to get her family off to a good start. She's not lazing about while she could be helping others.

In the context of the whole chapter, the idea that this woman reflects an impractical ideal for modern women falls flat. Far from being anyone's doormat, this lady was a businesswoman (16, 24), a mom (28), trustworthy (11-12), prepared (21, 25), physically fit (17) and even a fashionista (22). To be frank she sounds more like someone we'd like to have for a friend than poor maligned June Cleaver.

Giving up our barriers, we begin to see clearly how we might self-evaluate and obey. What if this week you committed to getting up early one day? Could you prep lunches for the kids for the rest of the week? You could write on their napkins or bake a treat for the week's lunch boxes. What if you took that one hour of sleep and turned it into breakfast? A weekend breakfast on a weekday? Pancakes instead of cold cereal gets everyone off to a great start, especially if instead of a bleary-eyed resentful mom, they got a smiling, warm one.

Does God command us to set our alarm an hour earlier? No, certainly not. But as we read, will we evaluate, will we let the Word burst into life in front of us so that we can learn to imitate this excellent wife and be excellent women ourselves?

These three things, reading defensively, without imagination and radically will combine to keep us from seeing ourselves and situation clearly. They will prevent us from applying the Word of God directly into our lives. Attitudes that prevent doing the Word are the attitudes of fools.

Individual Questions

1. Look at Proverbs 31:11a "The heart of her husband trusts in her." Now answer these self-evaluation questions (if you are single, think of an important relationship that demands trust from you—boss, parent, child, etc).

    A. What could you do to be more trustworthy to your husband?

    _____

    _____

B. Can he trust your advice to be selfless?

_____

_____

C. Can he trust you financially?

_____

_____

D. Can he trust your discretion? Do you keep family/personal business private?

_____

_____

2. Read Proverbs 31:17 "She girds herself with strength and makes her arms strong."
Now answer these self-evaluation questions.

A. What's your relationship with your body? Do you keep fit? A woman's health is crucial to her family.

_____

_____

_____

B. Do you truly believe that beauty fading with age is essentially meaningless? "Charm is deceitful and beauty is vain, But a woman who fears the LORD, she shall be praised" (Proverbs 31:30).

_____

_____

_____

C. How many minutes a day/week do you spend grooming (make-up, hair, mani/pedi etc)? How many minutes a day do you spend in prayer or Bible study?

_____

_____

_____

Group Questions

. . . .

1. What other passages immediately come to mind as Scriptures that are easily read defensively, without imagination, or radically?

_____

_____

_____

2. Pick one as a group and paraphrase it into modern language and your modern situation.

_____

_____

_____

As we work through these lessons, we'll be evaluating ourselves honestly according to the Word of God. This is a painful exercise and the individual questions may bring up sins that we need to confess to God. I urge you to stop and do that immediately as you are convicted. I also urge you to make your class a safe place to confess your sins to one another. In other words, your class must be free from the danger that what's said on Wednesday night will become Thursday morning's gossip.

Besides this honest evaluation we'll be looking to apply practically what we learn. We will not be fools, whose houses crash in at the first gust of wind. Rather we will be the wise women whose houses will stand because they are built on a solid foundation of obedience to the Word of God! ∽

CHAPTER TWO

OBEDIENCE

A Housekeeper or a Wife

The List

In the last chapter I told the sad tale of my teenaged Bible reading. Back when I was hopping out of bed in a frenzy to mark "read my Bible" off my mental check list, I was trying to obey. In fact, the last thing I wanted to do was to disobey God, but as an immature Christian I didn't really understand obedience. I imagined that obeying God was mostly a list of things I should or shouldn't do. Remember to pray for a minute before bed—*pleasing*. Miss church on Sunday for anything less than the plague—*displeasing*. My definition of obedience was childishly narrow.

My mom always told me that the most persuasive lies were half-true. Every mature Christian knows that Bible reading is important, that lying is wrong, and that God insists that we do certain things if we want to be pleasing to Him. Despite our fuzzy feel-good culture, which whispers that God wants us to be happy, we know God wants us to obey. So what's the problem with having a little list of "to-dos" to help us?

To-do lists are familiar to every wife. In fact, it often seems that the to-do list is as endless as it is repetitive: was dishes everyday, buy groceries every week, clean sheets four times a month. Our husbands should appreciate what we do: groceries, laundry, childcare; those things matter and make our households function. Let's be honest, though, a housekeeper could do them.

Every wife has imagined herself a maid, like Alice from the Brady Bunch. Yet there are striking differences. Alice got a paycheck. We get snuggles. She had a defined work day. We get kids crawling in our bed at 2:00 a.m.. Alice had her own life. We share birthdays, the flu, vacations, and funerals; we share life. Marriage catapults us out of ourselves into the sticky thing called family. Being a wife is about relationships, not lists.

Like a marriage our relationship with God has a set beginning (baptism). It also has repetitive, disciplined activities (prayer, Bible reading, church attendance) to be done and sins to be routinely avoided (theft, fornication, lying etc). And to extend the metaphor a little further, these are things people can "do" (at least in external form) without a relationship with God.

As a child I understood the commandments easily. Do some things and avoid others. I knew I should be kind. But when it came to seeing unkindness in myself or being aware of a perfect moment to be kind to others, well, my obedience didn't easily extend so far. I lacked both the love I needed (for God and my neighbor) and the desire to go beyond what was required.

If we want to really obey God, we must abandon the list. It fools us into thinking we're walking in obedience when we aren't. If we're still defining Christian life in an Alice-from-the-Brady-Bunch kind of way, we might not notice that we are no kinder, no more patient, no more noble of thought than we were before. We might not notice we're maids, not wives.

Full of Love

So what kind of obedience does God want anyway? If list-keeping isn't going to work, is it because it is an antiquated and graceless way, harkening back to the Law of Moses with its strict rule-keeping? In other words have we become "Pharisees?"

Why did Jesus condemn them anyway? They made all the sacrifices, brought all the first-fruits, and kept all the festivals to the best of their abilities. They were the strictest of monotheists—no idol worship for the Pharisees. Was the problem that they focused on the ritual rather than on the moral parts of the law? If they had honored their parents, refrained from murder, adultery and so on, would they have pleased God with their painstaking obedience?

No.

Despite the lists of rules, even the famed Old Testament law was a law of the heart. Jesus insisted that whole of the law could be summed up as

"'YOU SHALL LOVE THE LORD YOUR GOD WITH ALL YOUR HEART, AND WITH ALL YOUR SOUL, AND WITH ALL YOUR MIND.' This is the great and foremost commandment. The second is like it, `YOU SHALL LOVE YOUR NEIGHBOR AS YOURSELF.'" On these two commandments depend the whole Law and the Prophets" (Matthew 22:37-40).

Love was always the thing. Love for God comes first (often identified with the first four of the Ten Commandments) and is followed by love for our neighbors (expressed in the last six of the Ten Commandments). All of the sacrifices should have flowed naturally from the deep love the worshiper bore God; every moral restriction should have had its basis in a love of not only family and countrymen but as Jesus emphasizes in the parable of the Good Samaritan, of all men. Jesus was dissatisfied with the Pharisee's law-keeping because it was loveless.

Ezekiel 16 tells the story of God and Israel in a parable. God sees Israel as an abandoned infant, truly orphaned and left to die. He takes her in, provides for her every need, and when she is grown, marries her. However, she never returns His love, never recognizes all the good He did for her, prostituting herself instead. This sad tale reminds us that there should have always been a loving relationship between God and Israel. God initiated that love by choosing Israel and providing for her. Israel should have gratefully adored Him. Israel's obedience should have overflowed from the heart of slaves set free. But whether the problem was idolatry, immorality, cold self-righteousness, or a lack of integrity, the Law simply couldn't bring about the needed change of heart (For other detailed examples of how dissatisfied God is with heartless law-keeping see Isaiah 1:10-20, 66:1-4, Psalms 40, 50, 51:15-19, Proverbs 15:8, 21:3, 27, Jeremiah 6:16-21, and Hosea 6:4-7).

Individual Questions

1. What kind of sacrifices do the New Testament writers call for from us (Hebrew 13:15-16, Romans 12:1-2)? How are these sacrifices an expression of love and gratitude? What is one thing you could do this week to share or praise God?

2. Make a list of things God has done for you. See Ephesians 1 if you need inspiration.

Group Questions

1. Read Ezekiel 16 (this reading may need to be adults-only depending on your translation). Retell the story using Jesus as the husband and the church as his wife. Use your collective imagination to add modern details.

2. Compare the lists you made individually in question 2 above. Compile a class list with Scripture references to print and keep in your Bible. Let it inspire you to loving obedience.

God always wanted Israel's obedience to the law to flow from their grateful, loving hearts. Under the law of Christ, what kind of obedience does God desire? John, the apostle whom Jesus loved, has much to say about this.

If You Love Me

Having finished celebrating Passover with His disciples (The Last Supper), Jesus begins the after dinner conversation with a bit of Q & A (John 13-14). Thomas and Phillip have rather well-known requests—"Lord, we do not know where you are going," and "Lord, show us the Father." However Judas-not-Iscariot asks the question we need to consider: "Lord, what then has happened that You are going to disclose Yourself to us and not to the world?" (John 14:5,8,22). He is puzzled by this statement from Jesus.

> "He who has My commandments and keeps them is the one who loves Me; and he who loves Me will be loved by My Father, and I will love him and will disclose Myself to him" (John 14:21).

Judas wants to know how Jesus could make Himself known only to those who loved Him and not to the rest of the world. This is a tough topic (related to the indwelling Spirit of Christ), and we can certainly sympathize with Judas' confusion. However, the point Jesus is making is not difficult. If we obey Jesus' words, we love Him. The Father loves those who love Jesus.

To answer Judas' question, Jesus nearly repeats Himself, "If anyone loves Me, he will keep My word; and My Father will love him, and We will come to him and make Our abode with him. He who does not love Me does not keep My words; and the word which you hear is not Mine, but the Father's who sent Me."(John 14:23-24). The point is irrefutable: Loving Jesus means obeying Him. There is no separating love and obedience.

I have never met a person who labeled himself a Christian who wouldn't say that he "loves God." But I know lots of people who simply are not obeying God. Perhaps they are actively disobedient; perhaps they are checking items off their list, but not growing in their relationship with God; or perhaps they are trying to obey, but simply don't understand that obedience begins with loving God.

Individual Questions

1. Find more examples from John 14-15 where Jesus ties love and obedience together.

_____

_____

_____

_____

2. Read 1 John 5:1-3 then paraphrase it here.

_____

_____

_____

_____

Group Questions

1. How does keeping God's commandments illustrate that we love God's children (1 John 5:1-3)? Not sure? Check out Matthew 12:1-14, 15:1-14, 25:31-46 and Luke 10:25-37.

_____

_____

_____

_____

2. Explain the connection between 1 John 5:1-3 and Jesus' answer to the lawyer in Matthew 22: 37-40.

_____

_____

_____

_____

Walks, Excels, Abounds

So what if we do love God? What if we go to church, pray, read our Bibles and the grace of God is covering our stumbles (1 John 1:5-10)? What would God say to us about pleasing Him? The same thing He said to the Thessalonians.

> Finally then, brethren, we request and exhort you in the Lord Jesus, that as you received from us instruction as to how you ought to walk and please God (just as you actually do walk), that you excel still more. For you know what commandments we gave you by the authority of the Lord Jesus (1 Thessalonians 4:1-2).

The Thessalonians were already walking as they should and pleasing God. Yet rather than simply patting them on the backs, Paul reminds them of three crucial commands. Why? He assumes that they can be both pleasing God today and still have room to grow into obeying the commandments they received in Jesus' name. He wants them to "excel."

The first commandment to be considered is this, "For this is the will of God, your sanctification; *that is*, that you abstain from sexual immorality" (1 Thessalonians 4:3). God wants them to be holy. This is not the immediate soul-washing sanctification of baptism. Rather Paul urges them to go on cleaning up the mess sin made of their lives so that they become more personally holy. Specifically, he references several kinds of sexual sins (1 Thessalonians 4:3-8).

Few people think of avoiding sexual sin as an area of their lives in which they should grow. Aren't we either sinning or not sinning sexually? Yet Paul has a wider view here.

Although he first mentions "sexual immorality" (in other words all sexual contact outside of marriage), he goes to list two other things Christians must be careful to do. The first is that we must possess our "vessels" with sanctification and honor (1 Thessalonians 4:4). There is some confusion as to whether that means we must exercise control of our bodies (our vessels) so that all impulses and desires are appropriately channeled or whether we must treat our spouses (our vessels) in such a way as to demonstrate sanctification and honor. Regardless, this is far more challenging than simply avoiding sex outside of marriage.

The second commandment Paul has in mind is love: "Now as to the love of the brethren, you have no need for *anyone* to write to you, for you yourselves are taught by God to love one another; for indeed you do practice it toward all the brethren who are in all Macedonia. But we urge you, brethren, to excel still more"(1 Thessalonians 4:9-10). Although the church is already showing its love toward those in Macedonia (the region where Thessalonica was located), Paul once again instructs them to excel more.

For the final commandment, Paul uses the curious word *ambition*. He wants it to be their ambition to live quiet lives, mind their own business. and work with their hands. If a child told us that was what she wanted from life, we'd encourage her to dream bigger! Yet in this passage, Paul encourages them to "excel still more" in even this.

> But we urge you, brethren, to excel still more, and to make it your ambition to lead a quiet life and attend to your own business and work with your hands, just as we commanded you, so that you will behave properly toward outsiders and not be in any need (1 Thessalonians 4:9-12).

In three key relationships (with your spouse, among our churches, and in regard to outsiders), Paul is not satisfied with some kind of basic morality. He doesn't ask us simply to do no harm or to refrain from such moral miscues as adultery, theft, deceit etc. He demands that we obey in a growing way, an exceeding way, an excelling way. Obedience is not a simple matter of do and don't, but a matter of more and better, fuller and truer all the time.

Individual Questions

1. In what ways are you already fulfilling these three commandments?

   A. Sanctification _____

   _____

   _____

B. Love to the brothers _____

_____

_____

C. A quiet life, working with your hands and minding your own business_____

_____

_____

2. In what ways could you excel in them still more? Be specific.

_____

_____

_____

_____

Group Questions
. . . .

1. As you completed the individual questions, were you tempted to say that you were already doing well and did not need to improve? Why?

_____

_____

_____

_____

2. Were you tempted to think of others who needed to improve?
   Why is this a dangerous temptation for a person who is trying to read and obey?

_____

_____

_____

_____

Reading Better

Imagine a bride on her wedding day, glistening in all her finery. What is she thinking about? Dishes? Laundry? Paying bills? No. She's thinking about her groom, their love, and their new roles as spouses. The other things will be a part of growing together as a married couple, but they aren't the heart of their relationship.

The day we became a part of the Bride of Christ we weren't imagining that Christian to-do list either. We were thinking about Christ who died for us, the Spirit who was promised to us, and the Father who welcomes us. The items on the "to-do list" are necessary to be a growing Christian, but they are not the heart of who we are.

How, then, are we supposed to understand the connection between who we are and what we do? Paul answers this way.

> For by grace you have been saved through faith; and that not of yourselves, *it is* the gift of God; not as a result of works, so that no one may boast. For we are His workmanship, created in Christ Jesus for good works, which God prepared beforehand so that we would walk in them (Ephesians 2:8-10).

We are God's handiwork. He created us, and when we put Jesus Christ on in baptism, He re-created us. Grace is inherent in everything God has done: adopted us, chosen us, redeemed us, included us, and sealed us (Ephesians 1). We neither deserved or earned any of these amazing things. Each is the free gift of God. That's who we are.

And what do we do? Good works. That's what God crafted us for, what He prepared long ago for us to do. The items on the short list like "go to church," "pray," "read your Bible," as well as the items that don't often make the list like "fasting," "visiting the sick," and "offering hospitality to strangers" proceed naturally out of our relationship with God. We do what we do because we are what we are.

As we seek to read the Word of God better, we need to re-evaluate ourselves. That evaluation, as we have seen, can't be based on a list of things we "do" or "don't do." That kind of list keeping has never been pleasing to God. The first question is, "Who are we?" If we stand as children of God, then the next question is, "Do we love Him like we should?" If we do, then we'll be busy doing what He made us to do. ∾

CHAPTER THREE

HOSPITALITY
Welcoming the Savior

When we consider obedience to God, hospitality is not at the forefront. In fact, I'd have to stretch to think of the last time I heard a sermon, read a bulletin article, or attended a ladies' Bible class in which hospitality was the focus.

In the midst of rushing from task to task, hospitality seems either a luxury or a hardship. Watching Martha Stewart turn dinner napkins into swans or Paula Deen add a pound of butter and charm to a dessert, we find ourselves lacking. On the other hand, we are often bombarded by "opportunities" to be hospitable. Out-of-town relatives call to say they'll be in for the weekend, and we sigh. Our kids text to say they'll be bringing a friend over to spend the night, and we grumble.

We need a renewed commitment to godly hospitality. It is not a sphere of competition in which we are judged according to our cleanliness, cooking skill, and craftiness. Neither is it a realm of suffering in which we are constantly bogged down with visitors. Hospitality is actually another way we are privileged to obey God.

Hospitality – A Central Virtue

We don't think of hospitality as a cardinal Christian virtue. To us, being a Christian means prayer, praise, kindness, and self-control. Christians must love their brothers and their enemies. Of course, we ought to develop humility, be blameless, avoid evil, and give to the poor. Since we're probably not all that good at these basic things, isn't adding in something as minor as hospitality essentially useless? What if I said, in God's Word, hospitality is central to Christian life?

Let's start with Romans 12 where Paul details the kinds of behaviors that indicate a living, holy, acceptable sacrifice. These practical commands represent the person every Christian wants to grow up to be. Yet in between "contributing to the needs of the saints" and "bless those who persecute you, bless and do not curse" we find "practicing hospitality" (Romans 12:13-14).

A single mention may be a coincidence—but twice is a message. As the book of Hebrews draws to a close, the author details the way Christians can show gratitude to God for the unshakeable kingdom He has given us. The gratitude the writer has in mind is a practical thing, an "acceptable service with reverence and awe" (Hebrews 12:28). It isn't a feeling of thankfulness, but rather what we do because of what He has done. Beginning with loving our brethren, the author goes on to urge us not to forget those who languish in prison (Hebrews 13:1-3). Buried in the middle though, is another commandment:

"Do not neglect to show hospitality to strangers, for by this some have entertained angels unaware" (Hebrews 13:2).

If twice is a message, then three times is an inescapable command. In the book of 1 Peter, the apostle has the day of judgment in mind. In light of Christ's return, he calls on Christians to take their daily lives seriously. He wants them to be sober, prayerful, loving, and ready to serve one another as "good stewards of the manifold grace of God" (1 Peter 4:7-10). In that list, just between loving one another and serving one another, Peter says,

"Be hospitable to one another without complaint" (1 Peter 4:9).

Hospitality is key to what Christians do. It is in the middle of what it means to be a Christian. Along with the laudable virtues of prayer, lovingkindness, and praise is hospitality to strangers, teachers, and brothers. Yet it is a virtue that few Christians practice regularly.

Individual Questions

1. Do you practice hospitality? How often? To whom?

2. When was the last time you complained about offering hospitality?
   What was the source of your complaint? Cost? Time? Irritable company?

_____

_____

Group Questions

1. Define *hospitality*. Give practical examples of ways to be hospitable.
   Think outside the box. How can one be hospitable outside the home?

_____

_____

_____

_____

2. Are you convinced that hospitality is a commandment?
   Think of another commandment that is overlooked as frequently.

_____

_____

_____

_____

Hospitable to Whom?

Twice during His ministry Jesus sent out His followers (Matthew 10, Luke 10). The apostles/disciples serve as both forerunners and harvesters. In both passages, Jesus tells them to travel in an unorthodox way. He sends them out without luggage, spare clothes, or money saying simply, "The worker is worthy of his support" (Matthew 10:10). The ones sent by Jesus, journey like Jesus. Throughout His ministry, He was impoverished, homeless, and utterly dependent on the gifts and support of those around Him. So those He sent echoed His story. Though they seem remarkably like beggars to our faithless eyes, Jesus says they have earned that hospitality. However, earning it is a far cry from being able to demand it.

In the cities that receive them, Luke records, they should heal the sick, eat whatever is set before them, and proclaim that the "Kingdom of God has come near to you" (Luke 10:8-9). In the cities that refuse hospitality, the same message is to be proclaimed, but the disciples are to shake the dust off their feet in protest (Luke 10:10-11). The image might be of a city so unbearably foul that the preacher is unwilling to be contaminated by even the dust of the streets. Or perhaps the stinginess of the city is so profound, that the disciples should refuse to even take their dirt with them for fear of being accused of theft! Regardless of the symbolism, the effect is the same; the inhospitable cities are to be cursed.

Perhaps most telling for our purposes is Jesus' conclusion in Matthew 10. He acknowledges that the ones He has sent out are in a vulnerable position both physically and spiritually (Matthew 10:16-20). Then He explains what it means to be a disciple, ready to sacrifice everything, ready to take up their cross daily (Matthew 10:37-39). Drawing to a close, He says, "He who receives you receives Me..." The receiving Jesus is talking about is hospitality. Those who welcome the teachers Jesus sent receive both God's Word and God's Son. He goes on to say, "...and He who receives Me receives Him who sent Me" (Matthew 10:40).

Our Savior said that in receiving those who proclaim His message, we receive both Himself and His Father. Yet we might wonder at the real meaning of the word *receive* here. Couldn't it just be a metaphor?

Luke 19:5-8 records that Zaccheus rushes down from his sycamore tree, prepares to have Jesus for a dinner guest, and he "received Him gladly." In Acts 16:13-15, Lydia, meeting with her friends down by the river, hears the Word of God and accepts it with joy. As soon as she and her household have been baptized, she asks Paul and his companions to stay at her house. Lydia and Zaccheus "received" in two senses. They accepted the Word gladly and literally welcomed the Lord (or His representative) into their own homes. In both of these cases, their act of hospitality follows as a natural expression of their acceptance of the message.

To whom do we owe hospitality? We obviously should extend hospitality to those who preach the Word. Ministers, missionaries, teachers, and elders are all in positions where the work they do makes them laborers deserving of their wages (1 Timothy 5:18). Not only that but in as much as we receive their word for God's truth, we naturally should open our homes to them. Criticism abounds in these jobs. The simple act of hospitality is more than an economic gift. It is a profound encouragement to continue in proclaiming His Word. When we receive our leaders, we receive Christ.

Individual Questions

. . . .

1. Imagine Jesus is coming to your home for dinner. What will you do to prepare? What issues concern you? What would you like to talk about? How would inviting your minister or one of your elders to dinner be different? Would it be the same?

_____

_____

_____
_____

2. Who proclaimed the Word of the Lord to you? Have you received that person recently? Commit this week to a call, an email, a Facebook message, lunch, or a visit to thank her. Or if she is asleep in Jesus, tell her story to a person you love. Write your plan down here.

Person: _____

Way to receive her:_____

Date to do it: _____

_____
_____
_____
_____

Group Questions

1. Make a list of people in your church who proclaim the message of God to you. How does your congregation "receive" them? (Be specific: by dinners out, by dinners in, by a thank-you potluck once a year?) What other practical ways could you bless them?

_____
_____
_____
_____

2. Read the book of Philemon. Consider the relationship between Paul (the teacher) and Philemon (the one who received him and thereby received the Lord). What obligations does Paul say Philemon has? How does he expect Philemon to fulfill them? How does this relate to our relationships with our own teachers?

_____
_____
_____

Saints

Hospitality is one of the few commands specifically commended to Christian women. When Paul describes the godly widow who is worthy of the support of the church, he mentions that she must have...

> ...a reputation for good works; and if she has brought up children, if she has shown hospitality to strangers, if she has washed the saints' feet, if she has assisted those in distress, and if she has devoted herself to every good work (1 Timothy 5:10).

In her sixty plus years of life, she has offered hospitality to strangers and washed the saints' feet. We, too, are compelled to offer hospitality to both saints and strangers.

To fulfill its basic functions of worship, teaching, spreading the gospel and supporting the "workers worthy of their hire," the church had to have saints ready to open their homes. Our first description of the early church indicates they were eating, learning, and praying together in the temple and from "house to house" (Acts 2:41-47).

Acts also reveals that teachers often stayed with local Christian families as they traveled. Peter, as an example, stayed with Simon the tanner in Acts 9:43-10:23. The apostle John commends Gaius for receiving the brothers who seem to have been on a missionary journey (3 John 5-8). Paul also was occasionally a guest of new converts. In Philippi both the jailer and Lydia played host (Acts 16:15, 34). The teaching and mission of the church would have been nearly impossible without the hospitality of brothers and sisters.

Perhaps most telling, the young church met in homes, often the homes of Christian women. When Peter was miraculously released from Herod's prison cell by the angel, he went directly to Mary's house where he found the saints praying (Acts 12:5-19). Writing about his old friends Prisca and Aquila, Paul also greeted the church meeting in their house. Closing his letter to Colossians, he mentions the church meeting in Nympha's house (Romans 16:3-5, Colossians 4:15). The early church needed hospitable people because hospitality was an integral way that goals as diverse as fellowship, evangelism, group prayer, worship assembly, missions, and the teaching ministry of the church were accomplished.

Individual Questions

1. Hospitality was a necessity in the early church. Look at this list of functions. Record the passages that indicate that the early church was fulfilling these through hospitality. Take a moment and evaluate your own involvement in these aspects of church life.

   A. Fellowship _____

_____

B. Evangelism _____

_____

C. Group Prayer _____

_____

D. Assembly of the Saints _____

_____

E. Missions _____

_____

F. Teaching _____

_____

Group Questions

1. Look at the list again. This time record the way your local church is working out these aspects of church life. Do any of them involve hospitality? Have we lost anything by shifting the place and method of fulfilling them? What? Could it be restored?

   A. Fellowship _____

   _____

_____

B. Evangelism _____

_____

_____

C. Group Prayer _____

_____

_____

D. Assembly of the Saints _____

_____

_____

E. Missions _____

_____

_____

F. Teaching _____

_____

_____

Strangers

This idea of treating strangers with kindness and respect is as old as Abraham. He invited three unexpected strangers in for dinner and spoke to Jehovah (Genesis 18). Lot invited in a pair of angels and was rescued from the destruction of Sodom (Genesis 19:1-29). The Israelites are commanded in Exodus 22:21 as well as Deuteronomy 10:17-19 to show love to the strangers in their land. The idea of kindness to strangers is tied to other issues of "social justice" such as treating the widows, orphans, and impoverished with the respect and care they deserve (Isaiah 58, Job 31:31-34, Psalms 146:9, and Jeremiah 22:3). God extends His loving care to the alien and stranger and expects His people to do the same.

However, the Law does not have God's strongest words on the matter. In Matthew 25 Jesus discusses His return. He presents the vision of Himself on the throne passing judgment on all the world, dividing everyone by species—sheep on one side, goats on the other. However, when He begins to list the criteria by which He will divide them, His words strike like lightning. He will accept only the ones who fed the hungry, gave water to the thirsty, invited in the stranger, clothed the naked, and visited the sick and imprisoned. Why? Because when we receive the stranger into our home, we receive Christ Himself, and by extension when we reject the stranger, sending him away, we also reject Christ.

We owe hospitality to all these groups. We receive our teachers, elders, preachers, and missionaries as well and naturally as we receive the Word of God. We welcome our sisters and brothers into our homes as an integral part of the church's function. And we usher in strangers small and great since they represent our Savior.

Individual Questions

1. Have you ever had a dinner guest you'd never met before? How about an overnight guest? Can you think of a situation where that might happen in your life?

2. Think of three Bible stories where the hero/heroine was an alien and stranger. Were they welcomed and given hospitality or rejected and cast out? What happened to those who offered or didn't offer hospitality? (See Genesis 18-19).

Group Questions

1. What objections to offering hospitality to strangers immediately come to mind?

_____

_____

_____

2. Why do you think Jesus worded His command to us to offer hospitality to strangers so strongly? It is by Jesus' very definition a "salvation issue." Practically, what can you do this week that would "invite in a stranger"?

_____

_____

_____

Reading Better

Once, while visiting a church on vacation in Malaysia, we were treated not only to a fellowship meal of street noodles after Sunday morning worship, but were offered the precious opportunity to visit with a couple over breakfast the next day and eat dinner in a sister's home. We were welcomed, fed, and blessed despite being strangers.

That memory of overflowing hospitality has guided me as I have sought to practice hospitality in my own life. Even so, my brain has often churned with panicked thoughts:

* But my house is dirty!
* We don't have any extra room.
* We barely manage to feed the folks we have!
* I work.
* I don't have time/energy.
* I can't cook!

Yet as we've mentioned before, God expects us to be changed by the Word, not to allow our circumstances to prevent us from obeying Him. It's up to us to examine ourselves, see our excuses clearly, and think of creative ways to obey.

For example being unable to cook is a problem we can solve either by ordering in or learning to cook. The struggle with a small home is real, yet there are creative solutions. We've bought stacking plastic stools to have more seating for Bible studies, and we chose bunk beds for our daughter so that her sister could share her room if we needed space for overnight guests. Offering hospitality does not require a lot of money; you can make a pot of chili or chicken noodle soup from scratch for less than a dollar a serving. Preparing coffee and dessert is even cheaper. Most of us can adjust our budget to include hospitality, if we are committed to obey.

I write as a person who has been blessed enormously over the years by obeying God's call to hospitality. When we lived abroad, we hosted a house church. Our sisters and brothers salved our loneliness. We've had friends in for dinner, seekers in for Bible study, and traveling teachers we've never met before sleeping in a spare room. It hasn't always been easy. I'm an introvert and not the tidiest of house keepers. Yet, hospitality isn't simply a command; it's a tool in our hand to enable fellowship, teaching, and evangelism. Jesus insists that it is the way we welcome Him and by extension how we welcome the Father. Don't hesitate. Obey God, and see what amazing things He's going to do. ∾

CHAPTER FOUR

GENEROSITY
The Gifts of Gratitude

One day I sat at the kitchen table across from a young Asian seeker, Bibles open. We had been reading and studying together for months. Pointing to some verses in 2 Corinthians, she asked me if our congregation gave money. I explained our custom, carefully focusing on details like when and how and to whom.

She nodded confidently. I thought she understood until she blurted out, "So God will answer your prayers."

"What?"

"You give, so He'll answer your prayers, right?" She lived in an idolatrous (literally offering sacrifices to statues) world where one makes sacrifices of money, food, incense, or respect to gain the god's attention or favor.

It was all I could do not to cry.

She can be excused for all that she didn't understand. It was her first introduction to our Lord, and she was learning as fast as she could. But for many of us, the generosity of God and our proper response to it remains a neglected and difficult topic.

The Generosity of God

Talking with my young friend about why we give is not the only conversation on generosity and gratitude that has lingered in my mind. Several years ago, I sat across from a wide-eyed college student who asked, "Why should I thank God for anything?" He also came from a secular/pagan culture, and he wasn't being snide. "Everything I have," he went on, "I did for myself."

A serious question deserves a serious answer. Without referring to his adolescent way of thinking, I reminded him that he didn't make himself a boy, give himself good parents, nor provide the food that let him grow up healthy, bright, and strong. He may have studied for the tests, but the parents with whom he was gifted sent him to school. He may have exercised or made nutritious choices, but God gave him unmarred DNA and an undamaged body. Any success he had attained was directly attributable to his family foundation, his strong body and mind, and the fact that he was not targeted by a tragedy. The buzzword *privilege* hardly describes the truth: His whole life is a gift from the hand of God.

Ours is too.

From the moment before the moment Adam was created, everything Adam had was also a gift. Rather than speak Adam into existence, God formed him. He was the literal handiwork of his Creator. Stamped in the image of God, Adam received life and breath from God's mouth (Genesis 1:26-27, 2:7). Adam lived in the garden God planted. God gave Eden to Adam for his home, his food, and his life work (Genesis 2:7-15).

As if all that wasn't enough, God saw Adam's loneliness and planned a wife for him. Although He let Adam sort through the animals looking for a helper (not the only man to think a dog might be better than a girl), God knew from the start what he needed. Adam needed someone to be bone of his bone and flesh of his flesh. So He fashioned her as well. Then in a scene that calls to mind a father giving his daughter in marriage, He brought Eve to Adam: Adam's gift (Genesis 2:18-25).

Body, breath, life, image, home, food, work, and wife—everything Adam had was a palpable gift from God. Adam and Eve had spiritual gifts as well. God walked in the evenings in the Garden where they lived. They had an intimate and immediate relationship with their Creator that their descendants could only envy.

Adam and Eve's sin, however, caused them to lose some of their precious gifts. They would no longer live in the garden God grew. They'd find life, home, and food much harder won. Yet even in their disgrace, God reached out and gifted them with clothes (Genesis 3:21).

These creation gifts continue to be our blessings as well. Each of us, like Adam and the young man in the story, owe our body, breath, and intellect to our Creator. We have home, food, work, and clothes because God made it so. The world, sustained by His power and wisdom, continues according to the pattern He set in motion long ago (Job 38, Ecclesiastes 3:1-15, 2 Peter 3:3-7). To this day He sends the gift of rain on the just and the unjust, allowing the sun to shine on the good and wicked alike. Why? Jesus said it's because He loves us all even when we make ourselves His enemies (Matthew 5:44-46).

But if Genesis 1-3 is the story of God's physical gifts to mankind, the rest of the Bible is the story of the spiritual gifts God granted. In Adam and Eve's presence, God promises their Descendant will crush the snake (Genesis 3:14-15). Abraham, Isaac, and Jacob are chosen as the ancestors of God's covenant people through whom "all the nations of the earth would be blessed" (Genesis 12:1-3, 15). With Moses comes God's own self-revelation and the wonder of His revealed law (Exodus 34, Psalms 19). God grants them judges, prophets, land, and kings. They are God's true sons, so when they rebel, He punishes them (Hebrews 12:4-13). Echoing Adam and Eve's sad story, He exiles them not only from the land He gave them, but from their intimate temple relationship with Him (2 Chronicles

36:15-21, Ezekiel 10). And still He hints that restoration, reconciliation, and resurrection are just around the corner (Jeremiah 31, Ezekiel 36:22-37:28, Isaiah 65:17-25).

Finally in fulfillment of all those long ago promises, that He would crush the head of the ancient serpent, that He would bless the world through Abraham's seed, that there would be an eternal King and an eternal kingdom, He sent His Son.

> But the free gift is not like the transgression. For if by the transgression of the one the many died, much more did the grace of God and the gift by the grace of the one Man, Jesus Christ, abound to the many (Romans 5:15).

And if those gifts were too small, God had one more amazing gift in mind. He gave Himself again: His Spirit into the hearts of those who would receive His free gift. The gift of the Holy Spirit, promised in baptism, seals us as belonging to God Almighty (Acts 2:38-40, Titus 3:4-7, 2 Corinthians 1:21-22, Ephesians 1:13-14). The Spirit of God pours the love of God into our hearts (Romans 5:5). In fact, the coming of the Spirit was so phenomenal that Jesus said that it was to the disciples' advantage for Him to leave so the Spirit could come (John 16:6-7).

Individual Questions

1. What physical gifts have you received? What would be impossible without them? Are there physical gifts you have desired? Take some time today to thank God for His generosity in your life. If there are gifts you have lost or not received (for example mobility, a healthy mind, pain-free days), thank God for His promise of resurrection and a renewed and perfected body (1 Corinthians 15).

   _____

   _____

   _____

   _____

2. What spiritual gifts have you received? Read either Luke 1-2, Philippians 2:1-11, or John 20 and thank God for the gift of His Son. Then read Romans 8 or Galatians 5:16-26, and thank God for sending His Spirit.

   _____

   _____

_____

_____

Group Questions

1. How does Matthew 20:1-16 illustrate God's generosity? (If you find verse 15 hard to understand in the KJV or NASB, check out a less literal translation.)

_____

_____

_____

_____

2. Earlier in the chapter we discussed that God sent His Son in fulfillment of earlier promises. Fill out the chart to discover how God's covenants were complete in Jesus.

PERSON	SCRIPTURE	PROMISE
Abraham	Genesis 12:1-3, 15:1-21	_____
Moses/Israel	Deuteronomy 27-30	_____
David	2 Samuel 7:1-17, (see also Psalm 2, 110)	_____

PERSON	SCRIPTURE	FULFILLMENT IN CHRIST JESUS
Abraham	Romans 4, Galatians 3	_____
Moses/Israel	Matthew 5:17-48, Galatians 3	_____
David	Matt 1:1-17, Luke 20:41-44, Hebrews 10:12-14	_____

Principles of Giving

What is the proper response to God's immense generosity? Our response to His mercy is to be merciful. Our response to His love is to love our brothers. Our response to His forgiveness is to forgive those who sin against us. In response to God's generosity, we give.

Knowing we should give is much easier than doing so. What gifts does God want from Christians, and how are they to be given? Paul answers these questions in 2 Corinthians 8 and 9. We do not find echoes of the Old Testament's straightforward system of tithing based on the needs of the Levites and the service of the altar (Leviticus 27:30-33, Numbers 18:8-32, 2 Chronicles 31). Instead, typical of the differences between the Old Law and the Law of Christ, we find a set of principles instead of a strict policy.

Paul's Principles of Giving

1. First, we give ourselves to God (2 Corinthians 8:5). It is only when we are fully committed ("All in" as my daughters would say) that we are prepared to give. When we can say with David, "For all things come from You, and from Your hand we have given You," we are ready to begin (1 Chronicles 29:14).

2. Giving is a virtue in which to be abounded. Think about that. We can't give minimally or reasonably or occasionally. Instead we apply the same enthusiasm to our pursuit of generosity as we do to pursuing faith, knowledge, earnestness, and love (2 Corinthians 8:7).

3. We are enriched through the poverty of Christ (2 Corinthians 8:9). In other words we are spiritually rich because Jesus made Himself every kind of poor. Don't underestimate His poverty: He was born in a stable, became a political refugee in His childhood, and was homeless throughout His ministry. Ever wonder why He and the disciples were always going back to the "Mount of Olives" (Luke 22:39)? They were camping out; likely there was no money to stay in a Jerusalem inn. Refusing to give back in support of His work makes us graceless ingrates.

4. We are not to give by command, force, or manipulation (2 Corinthians 8:1-8, 9:7).

5. We give what we decide to give and do so cheerfully (2 Corinthians 9:7).

These principles make certain things much clearer. For example, we should view with deep suspicion leaders who demand, threaten, and manipulate our giving. On the other hand, if we feel unwilling to give, we should be concerned. Our lack of cheerfulness is not pleasing to God and reflects deep cracks in our relationship with Him.

Finally in 2 Corinthians 9:6, Paul gives them a much misunderstood promise. "He who sows sparingly will also reap sparingly, and he who sows bountifully will also reap bountifully." This has often been interpreted that if we give to God, He automatically returns physical blessings to us. This misreading is perilously close to the idolatry that began this chapter where sacrifices are offered to gain the attention or favor of the god. The bountiful harvest God promises in context is "sufficiency in everything," "abundance for every good deed," and a wealth of righteousness (2 Corinthians 9:8-10).

Individual Questions

1. Evaluate your own giving. Do you give weekly? In what proportion of your budget? Estimate your entertainment costs and compare.

_____

_____

_____

_____

2. Besides giving money in your local church, in what other kinds of giving are you involved?

_____

_____

_____

Group Questions

1. Discuss these questions: Is it wrong to tithe? Is it wrong to insist that others tithe? How can we guide young or immature Christians in giving cheerfully?

_____

_____

_____

_____

2. Other New Testament passages like Mark 12:41-44, Romans 12:8 and 1 Corinthians 16: 1-4 also talk about giving. Read them and add principles to the list from 2 Corinthians.

1. First, we give ourselves to God.   6._____

2. Giving must be abounded in.   7._____

3. We are enriched by Christ's poverty.   8._____

4. Gifts should be freely offered.   9._____

5. Gifts should be offered cheerfully.   10._____

When Our Hands Are Empty

With all the amazing generosity of God in view, I want to ask, "Do we love God because of His wondrous gifts?" In fact, I asked that question in a Ladies' Bible Class. One wise sister immediately responded, "Of course."

Since I was anticipating a firm, "No," I was taken aback. Thankfully I had the presence of mind to say beneficently, "Go on" (a teacher's trick if there ever was one).

"We love because He first loved us," she said (1 John 4:19).

She was right. We can't even begin to love God without the gift of love He gave first.

I should have asked, "Will we still love God when it seems that all His gifts have been withdrawn?" That's the question that underlies the book of Job. God points out Job's righteousness to the adversary who complains that the only reason Job is good is because of God's hedge around him. Job had every ancient blessing: health, children, good standing in his society, friends, wife, and immense wealth. Would Job still honor God if all those blessings were withdrawn (Job 1-2)?

Although Job never knew about the supernatural conversation that resulted in his misery, he still answers the question quite directly.

"Naked I came from my mother's womb,

And naked I shall return there.

The LORD gave and the LORD has taken away.

Blessed be the name of the LORD"(Job 1:21).

Forty-two chapters later, Job has not changed his mind. He has begged to see God face-to-face and demands to know what he did to deserve all this, but he has never cursed God or withdrew from Him (Job 19, 23). God honors Job's suffering by granting him the audience (though not the answer) he desired and restoring his fortunes.

Habakkuk, a 7th-century prophet, has a similar tale to tell. He protests that wickedness is everywhere and "justice is never upheld" (Habakkuk 1:4). God answers that judgment is coming swiftly in the form of the Babylonians. Habakkuk wails that they are even worse than the people of his own country, but his protests are of no avail. As the book closes, he is aware the tide cannot be turned. God is coming with all of Babylon as His outriders. So Habakkuk sings,

I heard and my inward parts trembled,

At the sound my lips quivered.

Decay enters my bones,

And in my place I tremble.

Because I must wait quietly for the day of distress,

For the people to arise *who* will invade us.

Though the fig tree should not blossom

And there be no fruit on the vines,

Though the yield of the olive should fail

And the fields produce no food,

Though the flock should be cut off from the fold

And there be no cattle in the stalls,

Yet I will exult in the LORD,

I will rejoice in the God of my salvation.

The Lord GOD is my strength,

And He has made my feet like hinds' *feet*,

And makes me walk on my high places

(Habakkuk 3:16-19).

When every source of food is depleted, when he has to just sit and wait for the day of distress, Habakkuk exults in the Lord anyway.

Neither Habakkuk nor Job accept things quietly. They cry out to God. They pray boldly and bravely call on God to be just. But in the end, when they don't understand, when they can't change things, they don't give up on God. They love Him anyway.

I have known people of God who like Habakkuk and Job have suffered great loss. Think of a full-time caregiver who can't go to worship because she's at home with a mother-in-law with dementia, a young person who is struck by an invisible illness (for example, MS or fibromyalgia), or a single mom devastated by bankruptcy. In such a situation, not only do we have to wrestle with God like Job and Habakkuk. But we soon begin to wonder if we have anything to contribute. The most obvious physical gifts of time, health, and money are gone. What part do we have left to play in our local congregation and the Kingdom at large? Habakkuk and Job still show us the way. To the church we offer the same authentic witness of faith in times of suffering that they did. We offer God our love, our trust, and all the hope of our salvation. These are the most precious gifts He ever gave us. He won't be sorry to have them back.

Individual Questions

1. In 2 Corinthians 4:7-18 we learn Paul is in a similar situation to Job and Habakkuk. Can you find details in the books of Acts and 1 or 2 Corinthians to explain what he's been suffering?

_____

_____

_____

_____

2. Think privately of a time when you've suffered the worst. Looking back were you more like Job (demanding to know why God was doing this to you, like Habakkuk determined to endure God's punishment loving Him anyway), or like Paul (convinced that God had such wonderful things in store that nothing you suffered mattered in the long run)? Did you turn your back on God? What drove your response?

_____

_____

_____

_____

Group Questions

1. Outline Paul's argument in 2 Corinthians 4:7-18. What good things does Paul see coming from his situation?

_____

_____

_____

_____

2. Who in your congregation is suffering? How is the congregation giving to ease their pain? How are you? How can we help them see they are a vital part of our community of believers?

_____

_____

_____

_____

Reading Better

Talking with my young friend from the beginning of the chapter, I struggled to explain. The idea that my giving could be to "get God's attention" or inspire Him to answer my prayers had never occurred to me.

Finally, I decided to tell her a story. "Imagine that my little girl goes out to the yard to pick flowers. Her tiny little toddler fingers will squish them and soon, her face shining, she'll offer me a crumpled little bouquet of weeds.

Is she somehow trying to buy my attention or get her way? No. I do everything for her: make her food, wash her face, navigate the wide and confusing world on her behalf. She couldn't pay me back. Flowers don't earn her anything. They are only valuable because they convey a message: 'Thank you' and 'I love you.'"

"I give back to God that way," I said. "He gives me everything and if I gave Him every last moment of my life, every financial and physical resource I have, it would be nothing but a shabby bouquet of weeds."

I urge you as your read your Bible to pay extra attention to the gifts God has granted you, both physical and spiritual. Let your giving be nothing more than the overflow of your gratitude—the regular giving back of the time, health, money, trust, hope, and love that have been poured out in generous measure to you. Not because God needs something from you, or because you need something from Him but because like a child with a bouquet of weeds you want to say, "Thank You" and "I love You." ❧

CHAPTER FIVE

EVANGELISM

Calling the Unchurched to Christ

What do we see when we look out at the world? Scrolling down our social media feeds, do we see agents of cultural and moral change—enemies who are destroying our way of life? Surveying our coworkers over the lunch hour or the girls in our Zumba class, do we see good folks just doing the best they can? Peering at the people on the street corner what do we see? Pawns in an economic shell game or perhaps individuals getting what they deserve?

Jesus saw people just like the ones we know and declared them distressed and dispirited, like sheep without a shepherd. Transformatively, He saw them as the plentiful harvest of God.

> Then He said to His disciples, "The harvest is plentiful, but the workers are few. Therefore beseech the Lord of the harvest to send out workers into His harvest" (Matthew 9:36-38).

Jesus' words call to mind a friend of mine. She has a beloved daughter who has been a missionary in a developing nation for the last decade—an almost unbearable sacrifice. But my friend writes, "The first time we went to visit her, I wondered why she wanted to be in this place. I went out on the street and saw the throngs of people. I knew these are God's people, and they do not even know God loves them and sent His Son to die for their sins as well as mine. I asked for forgiveness and again I cried and prayed."

She looked at her daughter and recognized a harvester. She looked at the cold dead eyes of the people on the street and recognized a harvest.

Who are the harvesters for whom Jesus asks the disciples to beseech God? Who is going to share His vision of the people not as enemies, good folks, pawns, or prisoners of their own choices, but as the valuable harvest of God? Who is ready to work in His fields and pray for more workers?

Who is responsible for evangelism?

In Matthew's Gospel, the disciples are responsible for evangelism. Jesus sends them to proclaim the good news and pray God will grant them more harvest workers (see also Luke 10:2). But what about now? A close look at three other New Testament passages will complete the picture of who in the modern church is responsible for calling the world to come back to God.

> The Spirit and the bride say, "Come." And let the one who hears say, "Come." And let the one who is thirsty come; let the one who wishes take the water of life without cost (Revelation 22:17).

Who does John say is responsible to call the world to come to Jesus? First the Spirit. This is no surprise because we know He inspired the Word of God. Second the Church, the Bride of Christ calls "Come!" The third phrase, however, is personal. "Let the one who hears say, 'Come.'" Anyone who is reading this book has in some way "heard" the Word of God. Since we have heard, it is our solemn duty to call "Come!"

Second Corinthians 5:9-11 presents us with a different perspective.

> Therefore we also have as our ambition, whether at home or absent, to be pleasing to Him. For we must all appear before the judgment seat of Christ, so that each one may be recompensed for his deeds in the body, according to what he has done, whether good or bad. Therefore, knowing the fear of the Lord, we persuade men (2 Corinthians 5:9-11a).

Paul begins by declaring that it is his personal ambition to simply be pleasing to God. Then he reminds us that all men must stand before the judgment seat of Christ and answer for their deeds. This terrifying thought, he says, is what drives him to persuade men.

As I read these words, I wonder what it is exactly Paul fears here. Is it standing in front of the judgment seat himself and trying to explain to Christ Jesus how he neglected to share the gospel that saved him? Or perhaps Paul fears the righteous judgment of Christ on those who have never known Him and in compassion reaches out to persuade them. In the end, Paul's motivation is irrelevant. If we know the fear of the Lord, we must persuade men!

Let's mull over one more Scripture.

> Now all these things are from God, who reconciled us to Himself through Christ and gave us the ministry of reconciliation, namely, that God was in Christ recon-

ciling the world to Himself, not counting their trespasses against them, and He has committed to us the word of reconciliation. Therefore, we are ambassadors for Christ, as though God were making an appeal through us; we beg you on behalf of Christ, be reconciled to God (2 Corinthians 5:18-20).

So many times God calls us to do what He does. He forgives and He demands we forgive those who sin against us (Matthew 6:14-15). He is just, and He requires justice in our relationships (Amos 5:10-17). He is merciful and desires that His children freely offer mercy (James 2:12-13). God is in the business of reconciliation. He sacrificed His own Son to make it possible. "He has committed to us the word of reconciliation."

Stop and think about that. God has a message for mankind: We are not permanently exiled but can be welcomed back into the presence of God. He left that good news in our hands to distribute. We are Christ's ambassadors. We appeal to the world on God's behalf. The whole scheme of saving mankind relies on our obedience.

Those who hear are responsible to call "come," and we have heard. Those who fear the Lord and know of His righteous judgment are to persuade men, and we know. Those who are reconciled to God through His Son are called to beg the world for Christ's sake to come back to God, and we are the reconciled.

Who is responsible for evangelism?

We are.

Individual Questions

1. Who was responsible for teaching you about the Lord? Did they reach out to you in fear for your soul or in gratitude for their own salvation? If you're not sure, give them a call this week and ask them. Don't forget to praise God for them.

   Neighbor in Laferia IX in 1957 Pastor Stevens

2. Read 2 Corinthians 5. Make an outline of Paul's entire argument.

Group Questions

1. Compare outlines of 2 Corinthians 5. Decide on a 1-3 sentence summary of Paul's point. Discuss what Paul wants the Corinthian church to understand about...

    A. The new creation (both now and in the future) _____

    _____

    _____

    B. Judgment _____

    _____

    _____

    C. The love of Christ _____

    _____

    _____

    D. Reconciliation _____

    _____

    _____

2. Think of the last couple of times an outsider (not a child of an existing member) was baptized. Who studied with them? Who invited them to church? Practically speaking who has been responsible for evangelism in your congregation?

    _____

    _____

    _____

    _____

But it's so hard...

We are responsible for evangelism. But we knew that right? So what is preventing us from being the ambassador Christ called us to be? The Old Testament prophets have some answers.

Jonah saw the horror that the Assyrians wreaked on God's people and the world. They were a terrifying juggernaut of a civilization—literally hooking their captives in strings like fish. He did not want to bring them warning of their destruction. He knew that if they repented God would be merciful, and in his fear, Jonah was merciless. He would rather run away and ensure they got their just desserts (Jonah 4:1-4).

Merciless, compassionless, pitiless, driven by terror—we would never be guilty of such things, would we? (For a clear answer to that question, look at the attitudes of American Christians toward Muslim evangelism here and abroad).

Or take Isaiah, Jeremiah, or Noah for examples. Each of them faced communities that did not want to hear their message. Noah managed to save only his wife, three sons, and their wives (2 Peter 2:5, Hebrews 11:7, Genesis 6-8). Jeremiah got thrown in the guardhouse and then into a muddy cistern for his troubles (Jeremiah 37-38). God told Isaiah from the beginning that his work would not get a good hearing (Isaiah 6: 8-13). They preached anyway.

Each of them faced more rejection and persecution than we can easily imagine. We wouldn't be guilty of feeling that since we may not receive a positive reception from our friends, family, or community that we are excused from trying to reach them with the gospel, would we?

Isaiah and Ezekiel provide examples of another troubling feeling. In Isaiah 20, the Lord requires Isaiah to spend three years naked and barefoot. This action was a message to Egypt and Cush (modern-day Ethiopia). Soon they, too, would fall to Assyria and be led away in full humiliation without shoes, buttocks bared. Ezekiel spent the better part of a year lying on one side, bearing the iniquity of Israel. He played siege to a brick inscribed with the word *Jerusalem*. Lying there, he had to eat bread cooked over a dung fire. It couldn't have been a proud moment in his life as the exiled community watched on (Ezekiel 4-5).

We haven't ever neglected to obey God's call to tell the world about Jesus because we were embarrassed, have we?

Individual Questions

1. Although feeling inadequate isn't one of the emotions mentioned above, it is a common reason that people struggle with evangelism. Read Jeremiah 1. Why does Jeremiah feel inadequate to bring God's message? Does God promise Jeremiah success? What promises does God make Jeremiah? What makes you feel inadequate to bring God's message? Did God promise you success?

_____

_____

2. What promises did God make to you? Starting with these passages, make a list. Feel free to add other promises that come to mind.

A. Acts 2:38-39 _____

_____

_____

B. Romans 6:8-10 _____

_____

_____

C. Romans 8:31-35 _____

_____

_____

D. Colossians 1:13-14 _____

_____

_____

E. 1 Thessalonians 5:23-24 _____ santified

_____ Faithful _____

_____

F. 2 Peter 2:9-11 _____ rescue from trials _____

_____

_____

Group Questions

1. In light of these feelings, consider the following Scriptures. Write one or two words to describe how these Bible characters felt as they reached out to the lost.

   A. Jonah 4 _____

   _____

   _____

   B. Isaiah 6:8-13 _____

   _____

   _____

   C. Luke 19:41-44 _____

   _____ *rejection* _____

   _____

   D. Acts 11:1-18 _____

   _____

   _____

   E. Acts 9:10-19 _____

   _____

   _____

   F. Acts 13 especially 48-52 _____

   _____

   _____

2. Besides our feelings what else prevents us from being effective at reaching the lost?

   _____

   _____

_____

_____

_____

Motivation

Embarrassed. Rejected. Reluctant. Inadequate. Scared. Sad. These emotional factors do make evangelism more difficult. But don't imagine that these are the only potential problems. Jesus told His disciples the hard truth. He was going to die and they'd be scattered (John 16:32). Following Him, He told them, was the equivalent of receiving a daily dose of capital punishment (Luke 9:23). He said His followers were no better off than He was: Those who hated Him, persecuted Him, rejected Him, and shamed Him would do the same to them (Luke 21:12-19, Matthew 10:21-25, John 15:18-25). So if we can't expect to always be successful or accepted, what motivates us to keep telling people about our Savior?

Compassion: We look out at the people around us and we see the havoc that sin is wreaking in their lives. Addictions, affairs, envy, greed, and despair break our hearts, and we want nothing more than to see them come to the peace that passes all understanding. We, like Jesus, see sheep without a Shepherd, and we can't help but tell them about the Savior (Matthew 9:36).

Gratitude: Looking back at those who were responsible for teaching us about Jesus and up to God who sent His own Son to die to redeem us, we are profoundly grateful. He just asked us to tell others how to receive the same forgiveness, the same peace, and the same joy. We have heard, and we must give the world the chance to hear.

Fear: We look into the Word of God and see the reality of hell. Jesus has the Bible's strongest words on the subject: "Do not fear those who kill the body but are unable to kill the soul; but rather fear Him who is able to destroy both soul and body in hell" (Matthew 10:28). We fear God because the day will come when having rejected Him for their whole lives, people will be rejected by Him forever. Like Paul, knowing the fear of the Lord, we persuade men (2 Corinthians 5:9-11).

Responsibility: Jesus told His disciples:

All authority has been given to Me in heaven and on earth. Go therefore and make disciples of all the nations, baptizing them in the name of the Father and the Son and the Holy Spirit, teaching them to observe all that I commanded you; and lo, I am with you always, even to the end of the age (Matthew 28:18-20).

God has turned all authority over to Jesus. Now the Rabbi turns the responsibility for disciple-making over to His disciples. We are His disciples; our baptisms are a solemn promise to that effect. Therefore we go out into a Godless world begging it to be reconciled to Him.

There's one more motivator, though; one we don't often consider.

Presentation: There will be a day when we will be presented to God. Think of it like an old movie where the herald plays a fanfare and then introduces each person coming into the party to the Host and the room at-large. Who will vouch for us before the King? Jesus will. Jude and Colossians both indicate that He is the One through whom we will be presented holy and blameless (Jude 24-25, Colossians 1:21-24). Yet there is a striking passage a little later in Colossians that hints at something more. Paul says this:

We proclaim Him, admonishing every *wo*man and teaching every *wo*man with all wisdom, so that we may present every man complete in Christ. For this purpose also I labor, striving according to His power, which mightily works within me (Colossians 1:28-29).

Paul envisions a day when he will stand in front of God and present those he taught. He didn't save them, that part of the presentation will always be Christ's. Yet in some crucial way, he is responsible to offer them to God. The Christians he taught are his hope, his joy, and his crown of rejoicing (1 Thessalonians 2:17-20). With all the power that God has bestowed on him, he is working for this one purpose: to have mature Christians to present to God.

Imagine if we stood before God's throne and said, "Lord, may I present to you my neighbor, Maria? She is my joy and crown. I taught and admonished her with all the wisdom I possessed. I'm so glad to present your daughter to You." What a glorious day that would be!

Individual Questions

1. Make a list of people you know who are lost. Start with family members, friends, and coworkers and expand outward. Stop when you get to people you wouldn't greet if you ran into them at Walmart.

_____

_____

_____

_____

2. Consider the list carefully. How many of these people have you made an effort to reach with the gospel? Invited to church? Talked to about your faith? Asked about theirs? Prayed for their salvation? Decide on an actual number.

_____

_____

_____

_____

Group Questions

1. Look around your congregation. Consider who has some connection to the congregation but is not yet a Christian. Especially think of spouses, adult children, friends who have been visiting, and parents of members. As a group, brainstorm and record the names.

_____

_____

_____

_____

2. Consider each of the motivations in this section (compassion, gratitude, fear, responsibility, and presentation). Which of these will motivate you to reach out to the people on your list? Start now by praying over the list, name by name as a class. Be sure and keep it for next week's lesson.

_____

_____

_____

_____

Reading Better

Our hearts ache when we look out at the world and see with the eyes of faith that the people we know, the people we love, are lost. We want to look away.

We imagine ourselves trying to talk to our friends about Jesus and we feel anxious, embarrassed, afraid, and sometimes even a little angry. We want to turn away.

We look into the mirror of the Word of God, and we see ourselves disobeying (neglecting to do) a direct command of Jesus Christ. We feel guilty.

My friend from the beginning of the chapter is the perfect example of this kind of tension. She knew how important her daughter's work was, yet she struggled to accept the sacrifices her daughter's mission work entailed. No grandmother relishes being on the other side of the world from a beloved grandson. No mother dreams of her child living without the simple luxuries with which she grew up. The sacrifice is real.

The lost are real, too.

We can't look away. We can't turn away. We must to confess our guilt and get busy obeying God. ∾

Body of Christ

Heart for the Lost
Develop relationships
Patient
People on their own journey
Pray unceasingly

EVANGELISM
The Call of the Church

I remember preparing for a gospel meeting in our congregation. One Saturday morning, several members of the church met early to go out and do some "door-knocking." I was old enough to go along so they paired me with my Papaw. He was a shy, steady, slow-speaking man of God. I walked down the street with him, nervously rang the doorbell, and stepped back so he could ask whoever hesitantly answered the door if they would like to attend the meeting or study the Bible. Although the memory is a warm one, I don't recall a single person who came.

This is not my only memory of evangelism. Like many young Christians I debated in a friendly way with the church-going young people around me about the differences between where I attended and where they went. I invited kids to VBS, camp, and worship. Lots came. As I grew older things didn't change. I kept debating mainly with other church-going people about the churches where they went and kept inviting my friends to visit our congregation both regularly and during "special" times like VBS or Ladies' Days.

However, I wasn't particularly successful in any of these efforts. Debates and invitations to church did not translate into people who knew, loved, and obeyed God.

I knew evangelism was my job. I wanted to do it. I was trying, hard! But it wasn't till years later that I began to see where things were going wrong.

Audience Shift

The church never needs to shift its message to fit the culture. Although solidly historical, the gospel is also literally timeless, established before the foundation of the world. Yet, New Testament teachers did not hesitate to adjust their focus and explanations as their audiences shifted. Compare Paul and Peter's most famous sermons. In Acts 17 Paul faced the logic-oriented, idol-worshiping Athenians. In contrast in Acts 2, Peter confronted the Jews who had slaughtered the Savior only 50 days beforehand. Peter's sermon has Old Testament quotes and current Jerusalem events. Paul's, on the other hand, introduces the

Creator, explains how He is different from the idols they had been worshiping, and uses quotes from their culture to back up his ideas (Acts 17:23-29). Different styles. Different illustrations. Same point.

Living in the Bible Belt in the early 1990s, the majority of people I knew had prayed the sinner's prayer. A mysterious few were Catholic or Jehovah's Witness. Like Peter, I was one believer in God Almighty's talking to other believers about how to serve Him properly. I shared a vocabulary with them as well as belief that we could go to God's Word for the solutions to our differences.

These days, however, the people I know have changed. I am more like Paul, talking to people who may worship an "unknown god" but have little or no real knowledge about the Creator and His Spirit-inspired Word. They are known as the "unchurched" because they have no real commitment or affiliation with any congregation or denomination. They make up a majority of the people outside the Bible Belt, and their numbers are rising dramatically even there. Just like Peter and Paul, we have to know our audience to reach them with the gospel.

For starters, the unchurched are impossible to pigeon-hole. They have a variety of beliefs and backgrounds. They may believe God made the world, but not according to the creation account. They may reject God, but accept angels and demons. They may be familiar with the Bible and accept it as God's Word, but never act on this purely intellectual belief. Their backgrounds may include religious parents they've rebelled against, no religious instruction whatsoever, faithful attendance of a denomination with which they are now disenchanted, or years of church hopping.

Because of this, we must listen and speak carefully. There is no one-size-fits-all approach. We must carefully define the terms we use. More than once I've heard someone say they believe in God only to realize that they believe in a vague grandfather figure in the sky. We may need to simplify some of our language. The church has long used specific theological words (some biblical, like *propitiation*, and some from outside the Bible, like *trinity*) to express complex ideas. To the unchurched, this is babble. We need to find ways to express these ideas in common English.

They also may not realize *why* the gospel is good news. Only a sinner longs for a Savior, and our culture has lost the concept of sin. It has been relabeled as disease, disorder, addiction, choice, genetics, or even as a virtue like courage. Thus Christians must carefully define *sin* as both the wrong we do and the good we do not do. We must honestly and specifically confess our own sin. Confession makes us more "real." It demonstrates we are forgiven sinners, not self-righteous hypocrites. Confession also allows our friends to see real sin and its consequences without accusation.

Like Paul, we must begin in the beginning. If we want to make disciples, we must introduce the Rabbi. Even agnostics or those who believe that there are many ways to get to heaven are fascinated by the story of Jesus. He is attractive, electrifying, and intriguing. This focus on Jesus is not only necessary from a practical point of view (many assume they are familiar with Jesus' story only to be shocked when they actually read the Gospels), but it reflects the earliest evangelists' emphasis. In their words Jesus is "the author and perfecter of our faith," our chief cornerstone and the head of the church (Hebrews 12: 1-2, 1 Peter 2:7, Ephesians 5:22-24).

Finally, our audience may be uncomfortable and unfamiliar with "church." Much of what happens during a typical Sunday morning will seem foreign to them. Thus dinner with a Bible study to follow may be much more comfortable and productive. Spending Friday night with a friend is so much easier than getting up early, walking alone into an unfamiliar building, being greeted by 20 strangers (or worse ignored by 100 strangers), singing unfamiliar songs, and listening to an incomprehensible lecture.

Individual Questions

1. Without opening your Bible, tell the story of Jesus as if you were telling the story to someone who has never heard it. Do this either aloud or in writing. Begin with why He needed to come; don't forget His incarnation, life, and ministry; finish with His death and resurrection. If you found it difficult to tell the story from memory, go back and reread a Gospel, if possible in one to two seatings. Consider sharing your retelling on social media.

_____

_____

_____

_____

2. Define the following words the way they are used in the Bible. Feel free to use a Bible dictionary or other tools. Be sure your definitions are written in simple language.

A. *Sin* _____

_____

_____

B. *Faith* _____

_____

_____

C. *Atonement* _____

_____

_____

D. *Sacrifice* _____

_____

_____

E. *Redeem* _____

_____

_____

F. *Inspiration* _____

_____

_____

Group Questions
. . . .

1. What percentage of your community do you think is "unchurched" (i.e., have no real religious affiliation)? How is reaching them different from reaching those who are following Jesus the best they know how?

_____

_____

_____

_____

2. Imagine that a friend who has been curious about your faith for a long time invites you out to lunch to talk. She asks, "Can you explain to me what you believe?" What would you say? Can you agree as a class on three to five things that you must mention?

_____

_____

Method Shift

We've assessed the changes in our audience. To move forward we need a method that meets two criteria. It needs to be as effective as possible, and it must suit us as women. Not only do we have a role in the church that does not include preaching on street corners, but as women we are relationship-oriented and well-suited to "friendship" evangelism. Such a strategy can be based on three words: Pray. Build. Invite.

Prayer comes first. When Jesus chose the apostles, He spent the night in prayer (Luke 6:12-16). Before Jesus asked the disciples who He was, a confession echoing the one Christians make at their baptism, He prayed (Luke 9:18-20). Paul and the elders of Antioch prayed and fasted as he and Barnabas were commissioned as Antioch's missionaries (Acts 13:1-3). Prayer is the prerequisite for doing God's work.

We must root ourselves and the people we are evangelizing in prayer. Paul begged the Ephesians to pray for him to be bold in proclaiming the gospel (Ephesians 6:18-20). This is the same man who was rescued from a mob only to ask to preach to them (Acts 21-22). If he needed to ask God for boldness, it can't hurt us to word such a prayer ourselves. Jesus also prayed for His disciples both immediate and future (John 17, Luke 22:31-34).

As soon as we have begun praying, we need to begin building. Jesus was "a friend of tax collectors and sinners" (Matthew 11:19). We purposefully need to build relationships with the lost. Genuine kindness and good works are the perfect avenues for making friends. Babysit for a sick coworker; take food to a neighbor who had surgery; have someone over for dinner or out for coffee; give them a birthday card. It doesn't have to be expensive or difficult, and it shouldn't be confrontational. After all, we're building a relationship to earn the right to recommend our Savior.

As we draw closer to the person for whom we've been praying, we will offer an invitation. This could be an invitation to pray about a problem she has been experiencing. We could invite her for coffee or practice the hospitality we mentioned in an earlier chapter by having her in for dinner. We may have a chance to invite her to enjoy the fellowship of our church family at a picnic, on an outing, or even at church. Best of all, she might let you open your Bible and help her understand your hope (1 Peter 3:15).

The three components we're talking about (Pray, Build, Invite) aren't really sequential. In the most practical way as we pray, we keep our eyes open everyday to see how God is going to open up doors and opportunities to reach out to those people. The opportunities we receive to build relationships and confess our hope are the providential result of our prayers.

Let's examine a couple of scenarios. Begin by assuming you've been praying for opportunities to share the Word of God. What would be your response in each of the following scenarios?

SCENARIO 1: Twice a week you deliver food from the local senior center to a shut-in. One day you mention your congregation...

You: "Yeah, we go to the church down the hill. They're great. Warm, friendly, kind. We love it down there."

Her: (Flat and dismissive) "I'm Catholic."

    A) Use this as an opportunity to discuss why you think the pope is wrong.

    B) Assume she's not interested and never mention it again.

    C) Try again later.

SCENARIO 2: In the midst of a tight schedule, you notice an acquaintance wearing a lovely cross necklace; you point it out.

You: "I love your necklace. Are you a believer?"

Her: "I am!"

You: "I'd love to talk more about that but I can't right now..."

    A) Assume that since she said she was a believer, she has been saved and dismiss the whole thing from your mind.

    B) Think to yourself that you'll have to talk to her more, but then promptly forget.

    C) Invite her to come over Friday night (friends from church are coming for fajitas anyway) so you can talk more!

I offer you these scenarios not as some kind of test but because they are my stories and my friends. It's what evangelism really looks like in my life.

In the first scenario, I smiled and said, "Oh yeah? Do you get out to mass?" (She hadn't been in years.) A couple of months later, I tried again. In the meantime I built a relationship with her week in and week out. I got a better reception the last time I tried, but our story isn't over.

In the second scenario, I invited my young acquaintance to dinner. She went on to invite another friend. Although they had both begun to believe, neither of them had followed Jesus in baptism. The Christians they met at our house were instrumental in teaching them about the Lord and how to receive His grace. Two precious souls were saved beginning with an off-hand comment and a dinner invitation.

Individual and Group Questions

For each scenario below, first answer individually. Then as a group debate the merits of each option.

1. A single mom walks into church on a Wednesday night. You greet her cheerfully and ask where she's from. She's new to the neighborhood and still in the process of unpacking. What do you do next?

   A. Sit down and strike up a conversation about how much moving stinks, things she might need to know about the neighborhood (like how to sign her daughter up for school), and how much you love your congregation.

   B. Offer to help her finish moving. Volunteer your skills as unpacker; give a couple of sisters the heads up so they can help, too, then pick up a couple of pizzas to feed the crowd.

   C. Find out if she's been going to church. Should she say she's been visiting here and there for a few months, ask if she'd like to have Bible study once a week.

   _____

   _____

   _____

   _____

2. You have some "couple friends." They're like you in so many ways. As long as you've known them they've affirmed that they believe in God and pray, but they don't attend church regularly. You want to reach out to them. What should you do?

   A. Pray for them everyday by name.

   B. Invite them to visit your congregation.

   C. Have them over for dinner and look for every opportunity to turn the topic to matters of faith.

   D. Give them a Bible and a copy of _Muscle and a Shovel_. Tell them after they've read it you'd like to talk about it more.

   _____

   _____

   _____

   _____

What to expect when you are expecting (a baby Christian)

Congratulations! We've begun to pray. We've made a friend who has agreed to sit down and study the Bible. Now what? In imitation of a popular pregnancy book, let's examine five things to expect when we are expecting a baby Christian.

1. **Expect to wait.** Nine months are required to grow a baby human, and that is not too short a time to grow a baby Christian either. I do not mean that it is impossible for someone to hear, believe, and be ready to obey God's Word in weeks, days, or hours. After all, look at the Ethiopian (Acts 8:27-40). I simply mean if a person has no background in faith, such speed is unlikely. Jesus' metaphors for the kingdom include farms, vineyards, and babies. In both agriculture and gestation, patience is a crucial factor.

2. **Expect to begin at the beginning.** Spanish teachers don't begin with an original copy of *Don Quixote*, and we shouldn't begin teaching people about God with dense and complicated topics either. Consider using Genesis, working through a basic time-line of the Bible, telling the story of Jesus, or studying a Gospel.

3. **Expect a lot of sin.** Lost people are lost in sin! Our Savior took His message to political dissidents (Simon the Zealot), to a woman married multiple times/living with her boyfriend, to tax collectors well-known for their cheating ways (Matthew, Zaccheus), and to sinners of every kind (Luke 6:15, John 4, Luke 5:27-31, Luke 19:1-10). Jesus certainly didn't receive a warm welcome from the Pharisees whose sin was less obvious. It is those who know they are sick who welcome a physician.

4. **Expect to hurt.** The parable of the sower declares that not every person who hears the gospel will respond, and even some who seem to respond will in the end be lost (Matthew 13:1-23). Jesus' example makes it equally plain that just like He was hated and rejected sometimes we will be, too (John 15:18-25). Evangelism hurts.

5. **Expect to grow.** Teaching the gospel teaches us to pray, study, trust, and hope in a whole new way. We'll become more patient, more loving, and more compassionate. We'll see the truth that "the word of God is living and active and sharper than any two-edged sword" (Hebrews 4:12). We'll find our place in the kingdom.

Reading Better

If you are really committed to being transformed by the Word of God, it's not enough to read it or study it; you have to practice it. And of the issues we've talked about so far, evangelism seems one of the most difficult to practice.

I'd like to ask you to close the chapter and your class today, not with more questions, but with prayer. Pray for boldness. Pray for opportunities for each member of the class to share the gospel. Last week you made a list of people in your church who weren't Christians yet, pray for them name by name. Then go home and get ready for God's answer. Remember to look for opportunities to serve and bless the people to whom you want to reach out. If you aren't certain about your ability to share the gospel, study up. God is faithful and longs for each and every lost soul to return! ∞

CHAPTER SEVEN

Encouragement
Confession, Confidence, and Hope

When my husband and I moved abroad, a lot of inconsequential things changed. Did we miss American luxuries like air-conditioned vehicles, while we hauled groceries a mile back to our apartment at a sweltering 104 degrees? We did. But those things didn't change us at the root.

However, when people with whom we had been studying started to become Christians, we were transformed. It was like becoming parents all over again. We taught them, fed them (both literally and in a spiritual sense), stayed up late with them, and worried over them. We still felt a real need for elders to be responsible for us. Yet somehow we were now responsible for these new believers.

Leaving them was terrifying. We nearly turned the taxi around the first time we tried to go on vacation. When we had to move, I cried for a month. Although like all children they have grown up, moved on, and are responsible for spiritual children of their own, we cherish them. We have always prayed that they won't somehow grow discouraged, despair, and turn loose of their hard-won faith.

What drives that discouragement? What should we be watching for? How do we protect them from the circumstances that cause Christians to give up? How do we protect ourselves?

Giving Up

Hebrews has the answers. This is ironic because it is the New Testament book about which readers have the most questions. Who was the writer? Paul? Apollos? Titus? What was his exact relationship with his readers? Was he their initial evangelist or one of the core of "circuit riders" like Timothy who worked with many churches? Where was the letter going? Asia Minor? Greece? Judea? Did it even start out as a letter or could it have been adapted from a sermon or a series of sermons? Yet clearly whoever the writer was, he agonized over the same questions I am.

He had people he loved, people who were his to encourage and rebuke, people he feared could somehow give up. He couldn't stand the idea that they might somehow let their faith slip from their fingers. Where did the writer get the idea this was even possible? I've had many conversations with friends who believed that the elect of God could never remove themselves from His light. Even those who know better often comment that if they could have only seen the miraculous work of God they would never fail. The young Christians the Hebrew writer addressed had most likely seen the Holy Spirit work in tongues, prophecy, and healing, still the writer was most concerned.

Why? Because he knew that the elect people of God had experienced Him in full and given up before. God went down to Egypt in all His power, punished the oppressors of His people, and rescued them dramatically. They witnessed the mighty work of God in the plagues, the parting of the Red Sea, and the shaking of Mount Sinai. The Hebrew writer quotes multiple times from Psalm 95 to prove this point: Despite all they had witnessed, the Israelites did not believe (Hebrews 3:7-11, 15, 4:7). Standing at the border of Canaan, they gave up their faith and failed to trust that God could bring them safely through the conquest. Forty years later, God saw every member of that original generation dead before He brought their children to His "rest"(Hebrews 3:7-11).

With this story in full view the Hebrew writer says this:

Take care, brethren, that there not be in any one of you an evil, unbelieving heart that falls away from the living God (Hebrews 3:12).

The writer knew that Christian hearts can be as disbelieving as Israelite ones. Such people, "crucify to themselves the Son of God and put Him to open shame," "trample under foot the Son of God," "regard as unclean the blood of the covenant," and have "insulted the Spirit of grace"(Hebrews 6:6, 10:29). God will not take that lying down. "It is a terrifying thing to fall into the hands of the living God" (Hebrews 10:31). Like any parent or teacher fearing for a beloved child, the writer used his strongest language to caution them.

He wasn't with them day-by-day. He couldn't be the encourager they needed; so in light of the danger they faced, he appealed to them to encourage one another.

But encourage one another day after day,
as long as it is *still* called "Today," so that none of you will be
hardened by the deceitfulness of sin (Hebrews 3:13).

Individual Questions

1. Do you have Christians for whom you feel responsible but who have left your care, such as your children, students in your Bible class, or someone you have taught the gospel? Take some time today to pray for them. Send a card, a text message, or leave a social media post to let them know you are thinking of them.

   _____

   _____

   _____

   _____

2. Who is a great encouragement to you? Think of exactly what that person said or did to encourage you, and be ready to offer such encouragement to others.

   _____

   _____

   _____

   _____

Group Questions

1. Read 1 Corinthians 10:1-13. How does Paul parallel Christians with the Israelites of the exodus? What caused God to destroy them? What warning does Paul give the Corinthians? How can we take this warning seriously in our own lives?

   _____

   _____

   _____

   _____

2. What would it look like if a Christian utterly rejected God? What does the Hebrew writer warn about such a person (Hebrews 6:1-8, 10:26-31, 12:25-27)?

   _____

   _____

Encourage One Another Day-by-Day

When we read "encourage one another day by day," we might wonder where to start. Why do Christians grow discouraged? How do we comfort them? Where do we point to help them gain the strength to go on? The Hebrew writer has answers. He explains not only the many circumstances that cause Christians to grow discouraged but shows us where all our encouragement is based.

He knows that the people of God grow tired (Hebrews 4). Our ordinary lives plus teaching Sunday school, running a youth program, and reaching out to the lost will wear us out. In the long term, years of service slowly drain our youth and enthusiasm. Where is our rest?

He knows that sometimes we are rejected, embarrassed, and reproached (Hebrews 11:23-27, 13:9-14). We've seen that, too. Families, friends, or spouses just can't bear the change as we give up sin and shift our attention to the kingdom of God. Co-workers despise us for not following them into self-indulgence. Acquaintances know we disapprove of their sin and reject us out-of-hand.

He knows that our growth might be slowed (Hebrews 5:11-14). We've seen, perhaps, we've been babies who needed milk far too long. These Christians started out down the narrow way, but their faith never deepened, their soil was shallow, and they didn't grow the way they should have.

He knows that sin deceives us (Hebrews 3:13, 6:1-12, 9:14, 10:1-4, 12:3).

He knows that our suffering cripples us (Hebrews 2:9-18).

He knows that death terrifies us (Hebrews 2: 9-18).

In the midst of all this discouragement, where are we supposed to turn?

To Jesus.

When death comes calling, we are no longer slaves to fear. Our elder brother became flesh and blood just like us and rendered the devil powerless. Death has no more dominion over us (Hebrews 2:14-15)!

When we suffer, we learn to obey in the same way that our Savior learned (Hebrews 5:7-10). The Hebrew writer reminds us that since we suffer, our Savior suffered, too, so that He could become our merciful High Priest. He needed to understand our temptations so that He could come to our aid (Hebrews 2:10-18).

When we have to face our sin head on, when we have to resist it to the point of blood shed, we know that our Savior's blood is powerful and effective.

"For if the blood of goats and bulls and the ashes of a heifer sprinkling those who have been defiled sanctify for the cleansing of the flesh, how much more will the blood of Christ, who through the eternal Spirit offered Himself without blemish to God, cleanse your conscience from dead works to serve the living God?" (Hebrews 9:13-14)

When we are ashamed, we know He despised the shame of the cross (Hebrews 12:2). When we are rejected, we go to Jesus Christ crucified outside the camp (Hebrews 13:10-14). When we are tired, we rejoice in the true rest that God has planned for us (Hebrews 4). Jesus, our merciful High Priest, is the answer. We often turn to platitudes in the face of people who are grieving, suffering, rejected, and tired. We say "things will get better," "God never gives us more than we can bear" (which is actually not in the Bible anywhere and stands in opposition to Hebrews 11:37-38), or "what doesn't kill you makes you stronger." But rather than these pithy bits of human wisdom, the Hebrew writer has one source of encouragement: Jesus Christ. He drank the full cup of human life—the joy and the sorrow, the rejection and the shame, the exhaustion and the death—and emerged victorious.

Individual Questions

1. Pick one of the following verses about Jesus, and write it out in your own hand. Put it in your pocket, tape it to your smartphone, put it above the sink where you wash the dishes, or on the mirror in your bathroom. Use this visual reminder to help you meditate[1] on the role of Jesus as our forerunner.

    A. Hebrews 2:14 _____

    _____

    _____

    B. Hebrews 4:15 _____

    _____

    _____

    C. Hebrews 12:1-2 _____

    _____

    _____

D. Hebrews 13:13 _____

_____

_____

2. Jesus faced the same problems we face, including discouragement. Read John 6 (especially the conclusion, vs 60-71). How did Jesus deal with His discouragement? How can we?

_____

_____

_____

_____

Group Questions

1. Examine the following passages and discuss Jesus' role in each one.

A. Hebrews 1:1-4 _____

_____

_____

B. Hebrews 2:10-18 _____

_____

_____

C. Hebrews 7:23-28 _____

_____

_____

D. Hebrews 12:1-3 _____

_____

_____

2. Storytelling is one practical way we can encourage others by pointing to Jesus. Think of stories (and write down the references) from the Gospels for each of these situations.

A. Jesus was tired. _____

_____

_____

B. Jesus was rejected. _____

_____

_____

C. Jesus dealt with those who weren't growing in faith. _____

_____

_____

D. Jesus was suffering. _____

_____

_____

E. Jesus was fighting sin. _____

_____

_____

Hold Fast

The writer points them at Jesus who is their brother, their High Priest, their incarnate God, and the One who went ahead of them in every way (Hebrews 2:10-17, 10:19-21, 1:1-4, 12:1-2) and insists they must "hold fast." He says they must hold on and never let go of three things: their confession, their confidence, and their hope (Hebrews 3:6, 3:14, 4:14-16, 6:9-12, 10:23-25, 10:35-39).

Puzzled? I was, too. Confession of what? Confidence in what? Hope in what? It is not immediately obvious what these are and how we should hold on to them, but a little digging will make it clear.

Let's start with the idea of our confession. We don't have a great English word to translate the Greek word the writer uses. Two words that might be used to translate it—*confession* and *profession*—introduce an element of confusion. We usually use *confession* to mean "to admit to wrong" and *profession* to describe a person's job. Basically these are words we use to talk about cops and robbers more often than to talk about Jesus.

The compound word, *Homologia*, is more like a modern mission statement. It comes from two Greek roots you probably know: *homo*—same and *logo*—word. Simply put, our confession is the words we all have in common: "I believe that Jesus is the Christ the Son of the living God." These are the words that Mary and Peter declared and the words we affirmed at our baptism (Matthew 16:16, John 6:69, John 11:27).

The writer calls them to hold on to these words and never let go. Why? Because Jesus is truly the great High Priest.

> Therefore, since we have a great high priest who has passed through the heavens, Jesus the Son of God, let us hold fast our confession (Hebrews 4:14).

The writer also calls on them to hold fast to their confidence. Not confidence in what, but in whom.

> For we do not have a high priest who cannot sympathize with our weaknesses, but One who has been tempted in all things as we are, yet without sin. Therefore let us draw near with confidence to the throne of grace, so that we may receive mercy and find grace to help in time of need (Hebrews 4:15-16).

Our confidence is in Jesus who understands how hard it is to live without sinning. He knows how much mercy and grace it takes us to get through a single day. He is not a harsh High Priest who can't understand how weak we are. He lived as one of us. Now, He welcomes us and stands ready to help. That's why we're confident. He's the One to whom we must cling.

Can you imagine if we didn't believe that He wanted to help us, that He had sympathy for our weakness, that He was willing to forgive us again? Without that confidence how could we do anything but despair and go back to wallowing in our sin?

Finally, we cling to hope. What is the hope the Hebrew writer mentions?

To answer this we need to take a moment and delve into Hebrews 11: the Faith Hall of Fame. As the writer works through the men and women who are the definition of having "faith to the preserving of the soul," he emphasizes that they did NOT receive the fulfillment of their promises (Hebrews 10:39). Abraham didn't. He was promised more descendants than the stars in the sky and got Isaac (Genesis 15). He was promised the land of Canaan and died only owning the cave where his wife was buried (Hebrews 11: 8-19, Genesis 23). Neither did the Israelites, who received some rest in Canaan but not the full rest God promised (Hebrews 4:1-11). The writer glosses for us as a conclusion, "And all these having gained approval through their faith did not receive what was promised" (Hebrews 11:29). Their faith was always, "the assurance of things hoped for, the conviction of things not seen" (Hebrews 11:1). They believed God would keep His promises regardless of whether they saw it or not.

That, too, is our hope and our faith. We believe we have received an unshakeable kingdom, whether it seems to be shaking in our day or not (Hebrews 12:28). We believe that the "God of peace who brought up from the dead the great Shepherd of the sheep" will raise also us on the last day (Hebrews 13:20-21). We can't let go. We have to cling to our assurance and our boast: Our God is faithful (Hebrews 6:11, 3:6).

Individual Questions

1. Read Hebrews 4:14-16. Leave your Bible open and incorporate the words into prayer. Let God know how grateful you are for our merciful High Priest, His grace, and the opportunity to come before His throne.

2. Finish these sentences.

   A. My confession is... _____

   _____

   _____

   B. My confidence is... _____

   _____

   _____

   C. My hope is... _____

   _____

   _____

Group Questions

1. When the Hebrew writer wanted to encourage the people he loved, he turned their eyes to Jesus. What else did he encourage them to do?

   A. Hebrews 13:15-16 _____

   _____

   _____

   B. Hebrews 10:23-25 _____

   _____

   _____

   C. Hebrews 12:14-17 _____

   _____

   _____

2. The Hebrew writer envisions crowds of witnesses lining the route cheering the racers on. Jesus won the race and waits at the finish line. As we run, he calls us to cheer one another on. (Hebrews 12:12-13). What is your personal responsibility to encourage others? What do you do that you consider encouraging? What is each congregation's responsibility? How could your congregation improve?

Reading Better

The Hebrew writer knows that even if holding on to our faith seems hard, Jesus has already done the impossible.

> But you have come to Mount Zion and to the city of the living God, the heavenly Jerusalem, and to myriads of angels, to the general assembly and church of the firstborn who are enrolled in heaven, and to God, the Judge of all, and to the spirits of *the* righteous made perfect, and to Jesus, the mediator of a new covenant, and to the sprinkled blood, which speaks better than the *blood* of Abel (Hebrews 12:22-24).

Notice the tense of the verb. The text says "have come." We are not waiting to be enrolled in the Lamb's book of life. We aren't hoping to someday join the spirits of the righteous and God the great Judge. We don't wish to be with Jesus. We have come. Just like the men and women of faith listed in Hebrews 11, we may not have the complete fulfillment at this moment in our lives, but the faithfulness of God is such that we can count each and every blessing listed here as already ours.

Although when we talk about receiving the Word and being transformed, we are usually talking about reading to obey, this time we are reading to discover our hope, our confession, and our confidence: Jesus Christ. With such a great High Priest, how could we give up or let anyone else give up either? "Encourage one another day after day, as long as it is *still* called "Today," so that none of you will be hardened by the deceitfulness of sin" (Hebrews 3:13). ∾

Endnotes

1 Meditation is simply thinking about God or His Word. Unfortunately, as a practice it has fallen into disfavor with modern Christians. This is probably because of its association with Eastern religions, which teach "emptying the mind." This is the exact opposite of biblical meditation, which is filling your mind with the Word of God. If you feel uncertain about this practice, check out Psalms 19:14, 104:34, and 119:92-99.

CHAPTER EIGHT

PRAYER

A Discipline for Relationship

Let's say two people were falling in love, or if that doesn't suit, a large and loving family adopted a teenage child. They need to get to know each other. How should they go about it?

This one's easy.

They spend lots of time hanging out together. There would be fun stuff like playing games or going out for dinner. There would be dishes or yard work to do. Late into the night, they would share the deepest desires of their hearts.

How do we "hang out" with God? How do we get to know Him as our Father? We spend time with Him. Being with His family lets us join Him in work and play. Reading, meditating on and memorizing the Spirit-inspired Word allows us to hear what God has to say. And finally prayer is the method that God has chosen to let us share our thoughts with Him. Our prayer life is both a measure of and the means to increase our intimacy with God.

Jesus' life of prayer

At the beginning of Mark's Gospel, Jesus visits Peter's house (Mark 1:29-39). Finding his mother-in-law sick with a fever, He helps her up from bed, making her well. Word spreads, and by dusk, a cascade of Capernaum's people are at Peter's house looking to be healed. While the tired household is still sleeping off the miraculous night, Jesus sneaks off to a quiet place to pray.

Jesus' desire to pray outweighed His desire to sleep.

Later in the book of Mark, Jesus' disciples were out teaching in the villages of Galilee. By the time they return, they have become minor celebrities in their own right. They don't even have a moment to eat, so Jesus urges them to withdraw and rest. However, by the time the boat lands, there are thousands of people waiting. Jesus (in an act of patience I find astonishing) spends the day teaching them. The disciples urge Him to send the crowds off to get dinner, but Jesus feeds them instead. After this painfully busy day, He sends the disciples across the sea of Galilee toward Bethsaida and spends the rest of the evening on the side of a mountain praying (Mark 6:30-46).

Jesus' desire to pray eclipsed His desire to rest, travel, or visit with the newly returned disciples.

One more story will serve to illustrate the point. In the book of Luke after the healing of Simon Peter's mother-in-law, Jesus decides which of His disciples will be His apostles and then heals a leper. The leper, despite Jesus' orders to the contrary, tells the entire countryside. The people flock to hear Jesus and be healed (Luke 5:1-16). Luke comments, "But Jesus often withdrew to lonely places and prayed"(Luke 5:16).

Jesus was uninterested in basking in His own glory (even though He is the only One with glory worth basking in). He'd rather go pray.

We know some of the reasons Jesus prayed. For instance, when He spent the night in prayer in Luke 6:12, He seemed to have been praying about which disciples to select as apostles. Yet there are many other hours of prayer for which to be accounted. Much about these prayers remains a mystery to us, yet the Bible does reveal one of the things for which He prayed. Jesus cried and begged God to raise Him from the dead (Hebrews 5:7). How much of God's long-term plan was left clear in His mind as a human? We're not sure. But He knew that He was headed to Jerusalem to die and that He was the Son of God, the Messiah whom God had promised to send. We know He felt the need to pray boldly begging God to rescue Him from death and to pray passionately with "loud crying and tears." And for this piety, the Hebrew writer declares, He was heard.

There is a huge gap between me and Jesus. I sleep till the moment the alarm goes off. Then begins the pre-coffee, post-alarm grumbling. Jesus healed people half the night, then got up early to pray.

He was able to sustain an entire night of prayer (Luke 6:12-16). I find my mind drifting after just a few minutes. Once, after I read a book on spiritual discipline, I did the experiment that the author suggested and tried to pray for just five minutes without stopping or letting my mind wander. Trust me. Five minutes can be a long time.

Jesus was refueled and refreshed in prayer. To my shame, I often find it one more chore on my spiritual to-do list. Jesus prayed "often in lonely places." I find it tough to get ten minutes alone to do basic grooming.

Jesus, who trusted God the most, prayed to Him in anguished tears. On ordinary days, my ordinary prayers are dusty and dry.

I desperately need to bridge the gap so that I can begin praying the way my Rabbi did.

Individual Questions

1. Evaluate your prayer life with brutal honesty. How often do you pray? For how long each time? Where? Is it one more activity shoehorned into a busy day? Do you turn to prayer for rest and refreshment?

_____

_____

_____

_____

2. Outline your day. Be honest about the time spent in entertainment (TV, reading, surfing the internet, crafting, hobbies, etc.) as well as time where your body may be busy but your mind is unoccupied (sitting in traffic, taking a shower, washing dishes, walking on the treadmill). Where could you find more time to pray?

_____

_____

_____

_____

Group Questions

1. What is a reasonable amount of time for a mature Christian woman to pray each day? Answer in terms of both time and frequency.

_____

_____

2. Read Hebrews 5:1-10 paying special attention to verse 7. What attitude did Jesus have? How are our prayers affected by our attitude?

_____

_____

_____

_____

Bridging the Gap

Both Jesus' habit of prayer and His attitude toward it out pace mine. Like any baffled student I want to raise my hand and ask my teacher to explain. The disciples beat me to it, requesting, "Lord, teach us to pray."

His answer has three parts: a model prayer, a parable, and an example. The parable, which is about persistence, goes like this: A man has hungry late-night guests in the era before the 24-hour Walmart. Being a good host and so-so friend, he high-tails over to a buddy's to ask for food. His friend has all the kids tucked safely into his bed (co-sleeping is not a modern convention) and the last thing he wants to do is wake them. He replies, probably in a whisper, "I cannot get up and give you anything" (Luke 11:7).

But the desperate host keeps knocking, talking, and begging until finally his friend gets up and gets him some food. Jesus insists that this is not pure friendship; the sleepy friend is annoyed into compliance.

Jesus teaches us to pray like a man beating down his friend's door in the middle of the night. My mind boggles at the words one might use to describe that knocking. Stubbornly? Obnoxiously? It's almost as if we were four-year-olds tugging at our Dad's shirt trying to get his attention while he's on the phone. The metaphor may not be so far off. We need God as immediately as a child needs his or her parent and can come to Him just as dauntlessly.

Jesus demonstrates this immediate need in His model prayer (often called the Lord's prayer). Matthew records it this way:

> Our Father who is in heaven,
> Hallowed be Your name.
> Your kingdom come.
> Your will be done,
> On earth as it is in heaven.
> Give us this day our daily bread.
> And forgive us our debts, as we also have forgiven our debtors.
> And do not lead us into temptation, but deliver us from evil
> (Matthew 6:9-13).

This prayer is powerfully urgent. Because we have recited it so many times as children, it is easy to let the immediacy of the pleas slip by us. The prayer begs for today's food and forgiveness; things we easily recognize as daily needs. However, it also includes the protection we need every day from both the evil that victimizes us and the evil that seduces us. These things may already be incorporated into our daily prayers along with "bless those in foreign fields" and "help the sick and shut-in."

However, the rest of the topics in the prayer are just as urgent. When we say, "Hallowed be Your name," we are echoing ancient Psalms that praise the holiness of God's name. Psalm 145, for example, teaches us that praising God is the work of "every day" and "forever and ever" (Psalm 145:1-2). Praising God is a crucial part of communicating faith to the next generation and evangelizing the nations (Psalm 145:4-7, 11-12). Praise in our daily prayers is no light matter.

The phrase "Your Kingdom come" may be confusing to us since the church as the kingdom of God has come on Pentecost. Yet we must continue to pray for God's kingdom specifically for the strength and unity of Christ's body, and for God to bring people into His church locally and around the world.

Finally, we have the request that the will of God be done on earth as it is in heaven. In heaven the will of God is done instantly, joyously, and absolutely. Our world desperately needs that kind of response to His will. Men need to repent, live righteous lives, and extend His mercy and kindness to one another. This, too, is an urgent demand. As we await the return of the Savior and face off with the ever-present reality of losing souls to death, our most dire needs include praising God and begging His aid in seeing His kingdom grow and His will done.

We pray these things persistently because we need these things immediately. Neither yesterday's food nor yesterday's praise is enough. We understand this at home. A little girl can't thank her mother for yesterday's peanut butter sandwich and expect that small "thank you" to cover the next three days of home-packed lunches. A man who asks his wife for a refill of coffee at 6:30 doesn't assume he needn't ask again at 7:00. Even in our intimate relationships "please" and "thank you" must be offered again and again as the situation arises. We offer our prayers in just the same way.

Individual Questions

1. In your daily prayers what topics come up regularly? What percentage of your prayer life is praise, thanksgiving, praying for God's work/kingdom, praying to be delivered from temptation, praying for things you want, and praying for others?

2. What is the longest period you've prayed about something? Is the time measured in days, weeks, months? What was the result?

_____

_____

_____

_____

Group Questions

1. Draw a pair of pie charts. In the first pie let each piece represent how much time Jesus spent on the topics in His prayer. In the second let each piece represent how much time you spend praying about common topics. How much do your topics overlap with Jesus'? How much do your percentages?

_____

_____

_____

_____

2. Discuss as a class a need in your congregation or your local community that is worth beating down God's door. Commit to pray for this one need every day this week.

_____

_____

_____

_____

Boundless

When Jesus told this parable, He summoned us not only to persistence but to boldness. Why does God, who created the universe, invite us to beat His door down? Why should we pester Him with our most immediate needs every day? Because His benevolence is boundless.

Have you considered the story of the Syrophoenician woman (Matthew 15:21-28, Mark 7:24-30)? Jesus escapes the crowds temporarily by going north of Galilee to the coastal region of Tyre and Sidon. A desperate Gentile women wants Jesus' help. Although she stands by and cries out for Jesus to remove a demon from her daughter, He flatly ignores her. She shouts until she annoys the disciples into asking Jesus to send her away. Then she falls down in front of Him and says, "Lord, help me!" He replies with this seemingly harsh explanation of His mission to Israel:

" Let the children be satisfied first, for it is not good to take the children's bread and throw it to the dogs" (Mark 7:27).

Her witty reply that even the dogs get to crouch under the table and lick up the crumbs finally earns her heart's desire and something more: Jesus praises her great faith (Matthew 15:28).

Faith in what? Of course, she believed Jesus COULD help her daughter. Everyone knew that Jesus could cast out demons and heal people. It's the very reason that the Pharisees wanted to get rid of Him and the crowds swamped Him daily. No, she had faith that He WOULD help her daughter.

She believed in Jesus' compassion—His willingness to help her despite her gender, race, and language. She believed that if she just kept shouting, His good heart would be moved to help.

That's the same belief that Jesus calls us to in prayer. We believe that if we just keep shouting, God's good heart will be moved by our prayers. This mother is a living illustration of the faith and boldness we need.

Immediately after Jesus tells them the story of how prayer is like beating down a friend's door in the middle of the night He says, "So..."

So I say to you, ask, and it will be given to you; seek, and you will find; knock, and it will be opened to you. For everyone who asks, receives; and he who seeks, finds; and to him who knocks, it will be opened (Luke 11:9-10).

These verses could lose their punch if we miss that crucial first word. Just like the man who needed to bang on his friend's door if he wanted food for his guests or like the woman who needed to stand and shout until Jesus was willing to hear her, we have to ask if we want to receive, we have to seek if we want to find, we have to knock if we want the doors to swing open. We do all these things in prayer.

How can we dare to do this? It is a daunting thing to imagine pestering Almighty God on His rainbow-encircled throne (Isaiah 6:1-7, Revelation 4). Jesus answers this way.

Which of you, if your son asks for bread, will give him a stone? Or if he asks for a fish, will give him a snake? If you, then, though you are evil, know how to give good gifts to your children, how much more will your Father in heaven give good gifts to those who ask him! So in everything, do to others what you would have them do to you, for this sums up the Law and the Prophets (Matthew 7:9-12).

If as parents we would never dream of betraying our children's trust with nasty tricks, why would we imagine God would? He is the Giver of good gifts, a Father better and more loving than any earthly one. Other passages combine to make it clear that this is in no way a blank check. Good earthly fathers don't give their children everything they want, and our heavenly Father gives His good gifts in accordance with our motives and His will (James 4:1-5).

Individual Questions

1. Have you ever fallen on your face in prayer like the Syrophoenician woman? What prompted your passion? Looking back, how do you see the loving kindness of God playing out in the situation?

_____

_____

_____

_____

2. Have you ever felt that God tricked or betrayed you? Can you think of a Bible character who felt that way? What shift in perspective helped you understand more clearly?

_____

_____

_____

_____

Group Questions

1. Compare Luke 11:1-13 with Matthew 6:5-15 and 7:7-12. What differences strike you? How do you account for them?

_____

_____

2. Could we pray consistently and boldly and still receive a *no* from God?
   Think about Mary and Martha's plea when Lazarus fell ill or Jesus praying in the garden of Gethsemane (John 11, Matthew 26:36-46). What do their examples teach us about being righteous and faithful in the face of a *no*?

Reading Better

Jesus was the epitome of "pray without ceasing" (1 Thessalonians 5:17). Not only did He live out that truth, He taught us to pray the same way. Yet the gap is clear. Jesus' discipline of prayer eclipses our pitiful efforts. He could pray longer, stronger, more passionately, and more often than we manage.

Crossing the divide is not simply a matter of praying more. It involves praying differently. He prayed passionately, loudly, confidently, boldly, and persistently. He taught us to take our ordinary needs to the throne every day. All of this was the outworking of His understanding of prayer, not as a chore to be checked off but as a child's plea for his father's help. Jesus' relationship with God sustained an amazing prayer life. Jesus' disciplined prayer life sustained an intimate relationship with God.

There should be nothing we long for more than to be close to God, to fully realize our relationship with Him as our Father. And for the Christian, there is nothing more crucial than answering God's invitation to ask, seek, and knock. ∞

CHAPTER NINE

PRAYER

The Power to Change

In this modern miracle-free age, the kindest skeptics think prayer is psychology in action. It's a time of quiet meditation, a way of honoring our faith or our forefathers, they say. Prayer does exactly what deep breathing, introspection, and counseling do. It allows us space for introspection.

I've heard some believers say something disturbingly similar. Those particular believers think God doesn't work in prayer anymore to heal, give wisdom, or change the course of nations. They believe He hears our prayers of repentance and forgives our sin, but for the most part they assume the world proceeds without Him.

Does that sound right to you?

Believers know that our prayers are directed neither up to an empty heaven nor in towards our aching hearts. Our prayers are directed at God Almighty, who made the universe from nothing and knit our bones in our mother's womb. Our prayers are interpreted by the Holy Spirit through the intercession of the Son and heard by our loving Father (Romans 8:26-27, 34).

Prayer is one of the most powerful forces in the universe.

Prayer changes everything!

God uses metaphor and story to explain things that are heavenly or hard to understand. For example to illustrate His relationship with His people, He uses the metaphor of husbands and wives and stories about kings and subjects. Similarly God explains prayer with a pair of powerful ideas illustrated in story and metaphor.

First, prayer is a conversation. Not a conversation between a lonely soul and a silent God, but a conversation in which God's mind can be changed. Think about that! Besides the parable about the man beating down his friend's door, Jesus has another parable about persistence in prayer. He says that once there was a widow who begged a judge for justice. She nagged him relentlessly until the unjust judge finally submitted to her will. Jesus concludes the story with this statement:

"Now, will not God bring about justice for His elect who cry to Him day and night, and will He delay long over them? I tell you that He will bring about justice for them quickly. However, when the Son of Man comes, will He find faith on the earth?" (Luke 18:7-8)

Abraham illustrates how a faithful person can talk to God about His justice. Because of their relationship, God tells Abraham about the coming destruction of Sodom and Gomorrah. Abraham begins to haggle with God like a housewife over her day's vegetables. He begs God to save the cities if fifty, forty-five, forty, thirty, twenty, and finally ten righteous people can be found. Abraham boldly begs God to play out this truth: God, who is the judge of all the earth, will deal justly (Genesis 18:16-33).

When Hezekiah was ill to the point of death, he didn't talk with God face-to-face. Isaiah visited with the news that Hezekiah wouldn't live through this illness. The king beseeched God to remember his integrity and wholehearted service and before Isaiah had left the palace grounds, God sent him back to say that Hezekiah's life would be extended fifteen years. Hezekiah and Abraham illustrate Jesus' principle: prayer is the power to talk to God and change His mind (2 Kings 20:1-11).

In a much less well-known metaphor, prayer is pictured as incense. Old Testament worship was a visceral experience. The worshiper touched, tasted, and even smelled. Incense was burned twice a day on the altar in front of the veil in the tabernacle/temple (Exodus 30:1-10). David borrows this beautiful image in Psalm 141:2. "May my prayer be counted as incense before You; The lifting up of my hands as the evening offering."

Incense was also burned on the highest and holiest festival, the Day of Atonement. The High Priest filled a "censer" also called a "firepan" (a hand-held incense burner) with incense and then went to the altar of the Lord and gathered hot coals to add to the censer. He took it into the Holy of Holies where the smoke and smell rose all around the Ark of the Covenant (Leviticus 16:1-14). This is the background for a second reference to incense as prayer.

Another angel came and stood at the altar, holding a golden censer; and much incense was given to him, so that he might add it to the prayers of all the saints on the golden altar which was before the throne. And the smoke of the incense, with the prayers of the saints, went up before God out of the angel's hand. Then the angel took the censer and filled it with the fire of the altar, and threw it to the earth; and there followed peals of thunder and sounds and flashes of lightning and an earthquake (Revelation 8:3-5).

The angel receives the incense, mixes it with our prayers, and the smoke rises before the throne of God. Then he gathers fire from the altar of God and fills his censer. This smoking mixture of prayer, incense, and holy fire is thrown back to earth. And what happens? The earth shakes, the lightening flashes, and the sky rumbles.

We understand that prayer increases our intimacy with God, but we should never imagine that this means it does nothing more. The saints beg God, and He changes His mind; He alters the future based on their requests. The prayers of the saints rise as incense before the throne of God and when mixed with His holy power, those prayers return to this world with literally earth-shaking force. Prayer is not the "least we can do;" it is God's invitation for His saints to join Him in changing the world.

Individual Questions

1. Have you been guilty of thinking of prayer as a last-ditch effort to solve a problem or a tool for dealing with anxiety? Do you believe that God can and will work in power based on the prayers of His children? Can a lackluster prayer life be a result of this kind of doubt?

_____

_____

_____

_____

2. There is much to learn about incense both as a prayer and in its specific use in the Old Testament. Re-examine the story of Nadab and Abihu (Leviticus 10:1-11) as well as the vision of Ezekiel and the Elders (Ezekiel 8) based on what you learned in this lesson. What is at the heart of God's complaint against these two groups of men?

_____

_____

_____

_____

Group Questions

1. Using the following Scriptures, make a list of things that God has instructed us to pray about. Each passage may yield more than one topic.

A. 1 Timothy 2:1-4

_____

_____

_____

B. 1 John 5:16-17

_____

_____

_____

C. 1 John 1:8-10, Acts 8:14-24

_____

_____

_____

D. 1 Corinthians 10:23-33, 1 Timothy 4:1-5

_____

_____

_____

E. James 5:13-15

_____

_____

_____

2. As a class, choose one or two of the topics and imagine what would happen if we prayed and God answered. Then take a moment and pray as a class about one of these topics believing that God will not only hear, but that He will answer powerfully.

_____

_____

Deaf Heaven

Imagine a great king who has been fighting a long war with guerrillas. They have no way to win, but he lets them continue fighting in hopes that some of them will accept his offer of amnesty. Daily his throne room is flooded with petitioners. First, there are implacable enemies who regularly ask him for favors on the one hand and stab him in the back with the other. Second, there are enemy soldiers seeking to surrender and looking for help. Also coming before the throne are his own citizens, each with their own concerns. Finally, the most common supplicants the king sees are his soldiers asking for help fighting the war. They need skill, armor, wisdom, power, and victory—all of which the king has to offer. Whose requests will he grant?

The enemy soldiers in the parable represent those who pray despite their rebellion against God. They have little hope of having their prayers answered. The proverb, "The LORD is far from the wicked, But He hears the prayer of the righteous" makes that clear (Proverbs 15:29). The blind man in John 9 echoes the sentiment when he defends Jesus:

We know that God does not hear sinners; but if anyone is God-fearing and does His will, He hears him. Since the beginning of time it has never been heard that anyone opened the eyes of a person born blind. If this man were not from God, He could do nothing (John 9:31-33).

So does God not hear the prayers of the unsaved or in terms of the parable, enemy soldiers seeking amnesty? He does. Cornelius is the classic example. Though yet unsaved, Cornelius is described as a pious, prayerful, and generous man. His life moves God to action; The King of heaven sends an angel, redirects an apostle, sends down the Holy Spirit in Pentecost-echoing power, and makes of Cornelius the first Gentile saint. All of this divine activity is a direct result of God hearing his prayers (Acts 10:4). Just as He proved to Cornelius, God is near and ready to hear those who repent (James 4:8, Acts 17:16-33 esp. 27).

Even citizens of the kingdom of God can pray unheeded. How? Our sin can hinder our prayers. Jesus insists the sin in our relationships must be resolved before we come before God (Matthew 5:23-24). Sin in a marriage, specifically being less than gracious to one's wife, hinders prayers. (1 Peter 3:12). When our prayers are motivated by lust, envy, and self-absorption, they are unheeded. God will not enable our sin via prayer (James 4:1-6). Praying with a heart full of doubt is also ineffective (James 1:5-8).

The story of the King and His supplicants is right. God will hear and answer those who are wholeheartedly searching for Him and His Son, but He will not aid the wicked (nor Christians) in wickedness. Why would a wise and just God arm the rebels?

Individual Questions

1. Which kind of petitioner are you: enemy, seeker,[2] citizen or soldier? Take a moment and examine your life carefully. If there is a break in your marriage, friendships, or relationships at church, deal with those conflicts right now (Matthew 5:23-24). If there is sin and doubt in your life, confess it and move on. Don't allow Satan to stop your prayers.

   _____

   _____

   _____

2. You have three friends who are praying for things that they have not received. Look over the scenarios and decide what to say to each friend.

   A. Susan, a friend from work, has a live-in boyfriend. She loves him and is afraid that he is going to leave her. She has been praying that he will stay.

   _____

   _____

   _____

   _____

   B. Joann, a young friend of your daughter's, wants a new cellphone. She has asked her parents who say her old one will last another year. She confides to you that she has been praying that God will give her a new one.

   _____

   _____

   _____

   _____

   C. Karen, your son's preschool teacher, confides to you that she knows that she needs to be more spiritual and as a first step has started to pray every day.

   _____

   _____

   _____

   _____

Group Questions

1. Look back over the scenarios and compare answers. For each scenario fill in a passage that explains how/if God hears their prayers and another that would comfort the woman in question. Discuss the challenges of telling the truth while being loving and encouraging.

What does God say?	Comfort
Susan _____	_____
_____	_____
_____	_____
_____	_____
Joann _____	_____
_____	_____
_____	_____
Karen _____	_____
_____	_____
_____	_____

Prayers that God Will Hear

What about the soldiers who come asking for aid in battle? They long to wage the King's war, advance His kingdom, and serve Him with all their hearts. Jesus Christ, the sword-bearing rider on the white horse, is their leader (Revelation 19:11-16). He was supremely confident that God heard and answered His prayers, yet He submitted every prayer to the will of God (John 11, Luke 22:41-42). In His worst moment, His own life (inarguably the most important life ever to exist on Earth) was entirely forfeit to the will of God.

Prayers, like Jesus', submitted wholeheartedly to God's will are the ones that are guaranteed to be heard and answered.

This is the confidence which we have before Him, that, if we ask anything according to His will, He hears us. And if we know that He hears us *in* whatever we ask, we know that we have the requests which we have asked from Him (1 John 5:14-15).

What do we mean when we say, "according to His will"? Is John really saying that if God happens to want it to rain and we pray for rain, it'll rain? Basically a roll of the dice? Of course not. The will of God is revealed for us in Scripture. Prayers focused on what God wants and what God promised will be favorably received.

For example, it is God's will that we do His work; it's what He made us for (Ephesians 2:10). So if like Nehemiah we see some work that desperately needs doing, we can confidently pray that God will help us do it (Nehemiah 1). When we come to God and beg to be put to work in His kingdom, we can be sure that He will hear and answer. However, this does not always happen in the way that the petitioner imagines. For instance, Paul would have gone on into Asia to preach, but was redirected to Macedonia (Acts16:6-10).

We can also pray like Jesus that God will glorify his Name in the world (John 12:28). Hezekiah provides us a beautiful example of this principle. When his country was in the direst straits, when the enemy blasphemed the name of God doubting His power to save, Hezekiah marched into the temple, spread that ugly letter down in front of the Lord and prayed that God would hear what the King of Assyria had to say. He concluded with these words, "O LORD our God, deliver us from his hand that all the kingdoms of the earth may know that You alone, LORD, are God" (2 Kings 19:19). Soon 185,000 dead Assyrians testified to the fact that God will glorify His name (2 Kings 19). Rather than bemoan those around us who blaspheme the name of our Father, let us turn to prayer!

Praying for the gifts God has promised is also fruitful. When we pray for forgiveness, we can be confident it will be granted because our merciful and faithful God promised to forgive (1 John 1). When we pray for wisdom, we can be confident we will receive it. God will honor His promise, we need only ask undoubtingly (James 1:5-8). When we pray for the kingdom to advance in our neighborhood and our world, when we beg God to help us reach out to the lost around us, we can know that we want what God wants: souls to come back to Him (2 Peter 3:9).

Individual Questions

1. Considering what you've learned about God's will, what aspect of it could you be praying for today? For example, do you need wisdom, forgiveness, and protection from temptation, or do you need to humble yourself and ask God to put you to work in His kingdom? Don't just answer the question; stop now and pray.

_____

_____

_____

_____

2. Pick one of the stories referenced in this chapter (Hezekiah~2 Kings 19, Nehemiah~ Nehemiah 1, Daniel~Daniel 2, Abraham~Genesis 18:16-33, Jesus~Luke 22:39-46) or one of these other wonderful stories of prayer (Hannah's prayer~1 Samuel 1-2, Solomon's dedication of the temple~2 Chronicles 6:12-42, Jehoshaphat~2 Chronicles 20:1-34, Mary and Martha~John 11) and read it carefully. Meditate on God's faithfulness in answering His people.

_____

_____

_____

_____

Group Questions

1. Look at the list of topics God asks us to pray about from earlier in the chapter. Which of these do you hear prayed about most often in public? Which of these do you personally pray about most often? Take a few moments as a class, and pray about the topic you feel is most neglected.

_____

_____

_____

_____

2. Share the prayer story you chose with the rest of the class. Share any observations you made as you read. What it would be like if we prayed like these men and women of God?

_____

_____

_____

_____

_____

_____

_____

Reading Better

When God's soldiers beg for aid in battle, He hears them. When the children of God ask Him to defend His good Name, He answers. When we ask for work, for justice, for repentance, for the church to advance, for forgiveness, or for wisdom, we can know that those prayers are mixed with fire from the altar and come crashing back to shake the earth!

This is not to say that we shouldn't pray about the daily things we need. In fact, Jesus highlights these immediate needs in His model prayer. Nor is this some method for manipulating God to get what we want. Instead it's an invitation to ally ourselves with the Father. His war is ours. In seeking His kingdom, we become soldiers He is ready to arm in battle, protect from danger, and send out to do His work.

Far from being false comfort or self-delusion, prayer is the power whereby the saints petition the Almighty to do the very things He is eager to do. In prayer we take a small step toward joining God in redeeming the world. ∾

Endnotes

2 Although I write assuming that my readers are already God's children, let me remind you that if you identified yourself as an enemy soldier looking to surrender, God is waiting eagerly for you to do so. Nothing matters more. Just like Jesus obeyed God, received the Holy Spirit and was declared God's beloved son, you can be baptized for the remission of your sins, receive the Spirit, and become God's child today.

CHAPTER TEN

CRUCIFIED

Sin in the Life of a Christian

A merica is currently obsessed with zombies, featured on such TV shows as "The Walking Dead." We shiver with delicious fear at half-rotted corpses preying on the living.
Yet I suspect we are simply not afraid enough. Not that we should all barricade our doors,
stockpile food, and prepare for an invasion. The zombie apocalypse has nothing on "the
walking dead" all around us.

Every day we see people whose bodies are alive, but whose souls are dead. This phe-
nomenon began in the garden of Eden; Adam and Eve walked around "alive" for the rest
of their natural lives, but were physically and spiritually separated from God. Paul calls
it the "law of sin and death." If you sin, then you die (Romans 8:2). Sin makes us all into
"the walking dead."

Sin is a hard concept for us to discuss. Not only are we ashamed and embarrassed, but
we stumble over the vocabulary. In formal situations we say sin is "missing the mark" or
"both the evil we do and the good we neglect to do." Talking about ourselves our language shifts to "I made a mistake," "I was sowing wild oats," or "I still struggle with..."
The problem is that none of these descriptions or definitions evoke the disgust, horror,
and misery that accompany sin.

As Christians we are relieved to have escaped the eternal consequences of sin. "There is
now no condemnation for those who are in Christ Jesus" (Romans 8:1). We need not fear
the fires of hell, but do we still have to fight sin in our lives? How do we do that? What
does God expect His children to do now that they are saved?

Not to be zombies anymore!

Sinners and Saints

Although we most commonly use the word *Christian* to describe a person who has been
washed in the blood of Christ and is walking in His light, this is one of the least used
terms in the Bible.[3] Three other nouns, *brother*, *believer*, and *saint* are used commonly.[4]

Brother is an obvious reference to our status as children of God and co-heirs with Jesus Christ (Ephesians 1:4-14). *Believer* is simply a description; Hebrews 11-12:1 and 1 John 5:1-5 make it clear that those who really believe are those who will overcome and be victorious in Christ. But *saint* is trickier.

Saint is commonly used in English to describe a person who has been attributed with the ability to answer prayers and do miracles by the Orthodox or Catholic churches. The New Testament never uses that meaning of the word. *Saint* is also used synonymously with "goody-too-shoes," which doesn't really help us understand the New Testament usage either.

Simply put, *saint* means "the holy ones." *Holy* is another tough word to understand. Think of it like china. We all have ordinary dishes—disposable ones that go in the trash, plastic glasses that go in the dishwasher, and chipped ones we use every day. But then there's china. It's valuable, different, set apart for special use. That's what we are. We were ordinary and have we been declared "different." Just like *brother* or *believer, saint* describes every person who is washed in the blood and walking in the light. Saints are called out of the ordinary masses by God Almighty and set apart by Him for His special purpose.

Are we saints now because we were once worthy of God's call? In 1 Corinthians 6:9-11, Paul makes it clear that those who are now washed, sanctified and "justified in the name of the Lord Jesus Christ and in the Spirit of our God," were once steeped in immorality (1 Corinthians 6:11). Or as Ephesians puts it,

> Among them we too all formerly lived in the lusts of our flesh, indulging the desires of the flesh and of the mind, and were by nature children of wrath, even as the rest. But God, being rich in mercy, because of His great love with which He loved us, even when we were dead in our transgressions, made us alive together with Christ (by grace you have been saved), and raised us up with Him, and seated us with Him in the heavenly *places* in Christ Jesus, so that in the ages to come He might show the surpassing riches of His grace in kindness toward us in Christ Jesus (Ephesians 2:3-7).

The holiness that makes us saints is given to us as a part of our new identity at our baptism. In the same way, we are given a family name at birth (Say "Bush" or "Manning") then are called to live up to it. Just because the saints are granted holiness doesn't mean we don't have to live up to it. God says to His children, "You shall be holy, for I am holy" (1 Peter 1:13-21). The Father would never allow sin to shadow any part of His light.

Individual Questions

1. Read 1 Peter 1:13-21. When Peter says in verse 15 "like the Holy One who called you, be holy yourselves also in all your behavior," what kind of things does he have in mind?

_____

_____

_____

_____

2. The opposite of the word *holy* is *profane*, which means common or vulgar. According to that definition, what is the most profane thing you do? How does it mark you like a common sinner? Why is it unbecoming of God's saint?

_____

_____

_____

_____

Group Questions

1. New Testament quotes, like 1 Peter 1:16, often reference complex Old Testament ideas. With that in mind read Leviticus 11 (focusing on verses 44-45), Leviticus 20:22-26, and Leviticus 19:1-8. What kind of laws are tied here to the idea of holiness? How did obeying these laws make the people of Israel holy?

_____

_____

_____

_____

2. Compare 1 Peter 1:13-21 with what we read in Ephesians 2 and 1 Corinthians 6. What is the message for sinners? What about saints?

_____

_____

Fighting Sin

Is sin the difference in a saint and a sinner? Yes. Sinners, which all of us were, are people who are enslaved to their sin. They may scrub, but they can't erase the stain. They may win a battle, but they have already lost the war. They are mastered by it. Saints, which praise the Lord we are, people who are slaves to Christ. We are washed as white as snow, and though we may lose a battle to sin, Jesus won the war.

Sin is hideous in a saint; it is a stain on the holiness that we are striving to achieve and a shame to our Father who calls us to His own perfection. Jesus concludes His revision of the Law of the Moses with this very idea: "Therefore you are to be perfect, as your heavenly Father is perfect" (Matthew 5:48). Jesus reviews each law and then calls His followers to a higher standard. The ancients couldn't commit adultery? We can't look with lust. The ancients were called to take no excessive vengeance? We have to love our enemies. And then in the middle, there's this:

> If your right hand makes you stumble, cut it off and throw it from you; for it is better for you to lose one of the parts of your body, than for your whole body to go into hell (Matthew 5:30).

Jesus suggests that rather than allow sin to drag us down into hell, it would be better to cut off our good right hands and pitch them away. Amputation over sin. These are some of the Bible's most drastic words on the subject of getting rid of sin. As we talked about in the first chapter, it is easy for us to read words like these and struggle to accept the Word meekly. Time for some imagination.

Imagine a young mother in the hospital. She's been sick for weeks and no one knows the cause nor the cure. Finally the doctor comes in and announces that she has advanced cancer. It started in the bones of her hand and has affected tissue up to her wrist. He presents her with a choice: amputation or death.

Sin is death. It kills. Narcissism kills relationships; despair smothers hope and jealousy strangles love. We know lust brings life-ending STDs; anger leads to murder; and the selfish ambition of entire countries causes famines. Yet more powerfully than all this, each and every sin severs our connection to God. He is perfect, sinless, shadowless, and we contaminate ourselves. He won't be infected.

That's the force of what Jesus is saying. Whatever we have to cut out of our lives to get rid of the sin, up to and including body parts, will be worth it, because we get to live. The Great Physician who presents us with this drastic cure didn't just lose a hand to defeat sin, He lost His life.

The Hebrew writer was contemplating the price Jesus paid for our cure when he wrote this:

> For consider Him who has endured such hostility by sinners against Himself, so that you will not grow weary and lose heart. You have not yet resisted to the point of shedding blood in your striving against sin (Hebrews 12:3-4).

The fight against sin is exhausting. When we have won a bout or two, it is tempting to sit down and declare ourselves the victors. We jab at sin, but we keep the gloves on. We might try to stop gossiping, but we still sit with the same catty co-worker at lunch. We may recognize our envy, but we still grind our teeth over our cousin's "perfect" life. The Hebrew writer has no time for this wishy-washy nonsense. Jesus faced sin and won by shedding His blood. We dishonor His sacrifice when we refuse to get our hands dirty.

Individual Questions

1. When you answered the question, "What is the most profane thing you do," how did you feel? Meditate on how Jesus fought sin (with His own life) and how He calls us to fight it. Then make a detailed plan for fighting this sin in your life this week.

_____

_____

_____

_____

Group Questions

1. Look at the conclusion of Chapter 1. The Sermon on the Mount is one of the most likely passages in the New Testament to be read so radically as to be nearly meaningless. Go to Matthew 5, and outline each of Jesus' revisions of the Law. Make a modern application for your own lives.

	LAW	JESUS' REVISION	APPLICATION
Matthew 5:21-26	_____	_____	_____
	_____	_____	_____
	_____	_____	_____
	_____	_____	_____
Matthew 5:27-30	_____	_____	_____
	_____	_____	_____
	_____	_____	_____
	_____	_____	_____
Matthew 5:31-32	_____	_____	_____
	_____	_____	_____
	_____	_____	_____
	_____	_____	_____
Matthew 5:33-37	_____	_____	_____
	_____	_____	_____
	_____	_____	_____
	_____	_____	_____
Matthew 5:38-42	_____	_____	_____
	_____	_____	_____
	_____	_____	_____
	_____	_____	_____
Matthew 5:43-48	_____	_____	_____
	_____	_____	_____
	_____	_____	_____
	_____	_____	_____

Sword and Shield

We have discovered that we are the saints, set apart by God for His special purposes. We are called to live out that holiness in our everyday lives because God is holy and because His Son was sinless. We are to fight sin as drastically as a man willing to cut off his good right hand; as bloodily as man having gone 10 rounds before being declared the winner. With what are we fighting? What weapons or armor do we possess? Are we cannon fodder? Naked soldiers sent out to die?

No.

In the book of Isaiah, God sends His representative called "the Servant" or "the Branch" to bring justice and heal the people. This representative is Jesus coming in full armor as a mighty warrior. He is wrapped in a belt of righteousness (Isaiah 11:5). His Word is a weapon of enormous power (Isaiah 11:4, Isaiah 49:2). He bears the breastplate of righteousness and the helmet of salvation. Billowing behind Him is a mantle of zeal and His clothing is vengeance (Isaiah 59:17).

The Gospels show Jesus in His armor. His breastplate of righteousness was so profound that they struggled to find people able to lie about him effectively (Matthew 26:59-64). He wrapped Himself in absolute truth; in both inconvenient moments and life-threatening ones, He confessed that He was the Messiah, the Son of God (Matthew 26:63-64). He wore the helmet of salvation both calling others to be saved from this world and in assurance that He would be saved from the power of death.

And His weapon? The Sword of the Spirit is the "Word of God." When Jesus had to face the devil in the wilderness, He quoted God's Word as His reply. Did you ever wonder how He parried so skillfully? There was no pocket concordance; He had committed those verses to memory. He also spoke with authority as the oracle of God wielding the Word in story, parable, and prayer (Mark 1:22). He had long, slow conversations with the most unexpected people (John 3, 4). Words were always His weapon of choice.

Saint-soldiers are sent out according to Paul in Ephesians 6:10-17 wearing the armor of their King. Our armor is given to us for one purpose: that we may "be able to stand firm against the schemes of the devil" (Ephesians 6:11). It's an armor made for facing the enemy and resisting Satan so that he will flee from us (James 4:7). It is God's own armor, worn by His Son and graced to us.

Paul explains what God's soldiers are battling. We combat "the spiritual *forces* of wickedness in the heavenly *places*" (Ephesians 6:12). We are not at war with governments—ours or foreign. The lost are not our enemies either. They are the POWs we long to save. We campaign against the darkness.

In our own lives, darkness is battled by shining light on our sin. Sin grows in the dark and feeds on deception. Confession is one of God's most powerful flashlights. Go to God in prayer and pray honestly. Not "Lord, forgive me of all my sin" but an honest description of what happened. As in…

"Lord, I wanted five quiet minutes by myself. In my selfish desire I snapped at my husband when he interrupted me. I let my resentment brew and didn't control my thoughts for the rest of the day. I know I hurt him. I asked his forgiveness, and I ask You to please forgive me, too."

Then go to a trusted believer (an elder; a wise, older lady; or a godly young sister) and tell that person the truth. Confession serves a dual purpose. The love and prayers of our sisters and brothers help us overcome the sin we confess. And when we tell the truth about our sin, we invite others to do so as well. Soon we discover that we are not alone in the darkness.

Our armor is the gift of our warrior King. How do we win the battle against Satan? With the shield of faith, we defeat sin in our lives. "Having shod our feet with the preparation of the gospel of peace" (Ephesians 6:15), we bring good news to the lost. We stand as soldiers of God blameless in our breastplate of righteousness and wrapped in integrity. Although the devil is ultimately defeated in the war, whether or not he wins the battle for our lives (and the lives of those we touch) depends on how we use our armor today.

Therefore, take up the full armor of God, so that you will be able to resist in the evil day, and having done everything, to stand firm (Ephesians 6:13).

Individual Questions

1. Reread Isaiah 11:1-10, Isaiah 49:1-13, and Isaiah 59. Picture Jesus as He is described with either a paragraph, a poem, or a picture. What did you learn about Jesus? How can we imitate Him as He's depicted in these verses?

_____

_____

_____

_____

2. Jesus defeated Satan with the Word of God. We need to have the Word in our minds, our hearts, and our mouths (not just on our smartphones) so that we can be ready to battle him. Choose a verse that relates to the sin you made a plan to defeat. Write it on a piece

of paper, stick it in your pocket, and commit to reading it every day this week. The Word of God will help you battle temptation!

_____

_____

_____

_____

Group Questions

1. Discuss how you think of yourselves. In your own eyes are you soldiers wrapped in the armor of Jesus Christ? Or saints, daily becoming holy as our Father is holy? How does our image of ourselves effect our daily behavior? How are we damaged by a false perspective; for example, thinking of ourselves as wretched sinners rather than holy soldiers?

_____

_____

_____

_____

2. Read 1 Corinthians 15:50-58. When does Paul say we have the victory here? Over what do we have victory? Who do we have to thank for this victory?

_____

_____

_____

_____

Reading Better

Sin is a powerful enemy. Even when sin is no longer our master, Jesus suggests that it is dangerous enough that it would be better to cut off a body part than allow it to have sway in our lives.

I wish sin didn't still plague us. I wish we could live every day as holy in our thoughts and behavior as God has made us in Christ Jesus.

Yet we are not defeated sinners: miserable slaves to a cruel master. We are not zombies walking around spiritually dead. We are the victors because our Savior was victorious.

We are encased in His armor. We are armed with His sword. The challenge today and every day is to live up to the gift of victory He offers us. ∾

Endnotes

3 "Christian" is used twice in Acts and once in 1 Peter (Acts 11:26, 26:28 and 1 Peter 4:16).

4 For example, the word *brother* is used in 1 Corinthians 6:6, 8:11-13, Colossians 4:7-9, Phile-mon 1:7,16, and 1 Peter 5:12 and "believer" in Acts 10:45, 16:1, 2 Corinthians 6:15, 1 Timothy 4:10, 5:16, 6:2.

CHAPTER ELEVEN

RELATIONSHIPS

Single, Married, and Single Again

Little girls love princesses. Tulle and high heels, midnight dances and handsome princes paint a charming vision. These fairy tales inform our cultural sub-conscience. For every girl there is a rich, handsome man to come charging in and rescue her from her hard work and mundane life.

Although feminists roundly reject this vision, Christians should protest it all the more. Godly wives are competent and devoted partners, not helpless princesses. The most important characteristics of a marriage are faithfulness, constancy, and committed love. The curtain of "happily ever after" falling over a departing couple headed for their honeymoon is, at best, unrealistic or, at worst, a flat lie. Not only is it a false vision of life as a wife, it is frequently a false future.

The church in Corinth had questions about Christian families. For instance, can married Christians have sex? If one partner in a marriage became a Christian but the other didn't, are they still really married? What about the kids? What about singles? What about widows? They contacted Paul whose answers reveal much about not only the Corinthian situation but ours as well.

God has plans for His daughters in every season and every circumstance of their lives. He intends to be their true fulfillment, not send a man to do the job. Single, married, or single again, God has a place in His kingdom for every woman. That's the true story of what it means to be a princess—a daughter of the King.

Single

God's vision for His single girls is quite different from either the vision of the world or the vision of the church. The story that the world tells about being "single" is a time of being young. On the upside there are parties, karaoke nights, and long weekends hanging out with friends. There are "wild oats" to be sown in terms of both hangovers and regrettable boyfriends. On the downside, there are lots of heartbreaks complete with the stereotypical tears and ice cream. However, the world has an ugly cutoff. At a certain age, she becomes an "Old Maid." All her friends have paired off and had their fairytale weddings, but she is left single and old with dozens of cats to keep her company.

In the church the vision is scarcely better. "Single" has become a time of waiting. The ultimate destiny of every girl is to be a wife and mom. She has a few short years to look, wait, and then take her place among the fulfilled. During this time she is relegated to the "young professionals" class or stuck lingering in the "college-aged class." Eventually she might be pushed to the "singles" class where, as everyone knows, old dinosaurs go to die.

Although I'll admit to some satire here, both the church and the world belittle singles. Paul, himself without a wife at least at this stage of his life, has an entirely different outlook. He whole-heartedly recommends being single. Writing at a time when persecution was about to become a decision-making factor at every level of a Christian's life (he calls it the "present distress" in 1 Corinthians 7:26), he suggests that they would all be better off if they were unwed. It takes little imagination to see how a single woman fleeing persecution would have advantages over a hugely pregnant or nursing mother.

Moreover, he sees a powerful positive in the single life-freedom.

But I want you to be free from concern. One who is unmarried is concerned about the things of the Lord, how he may please the Lord; but one who is married is concerned about the things of the world, how he may please his wife, and *his interests* are divided. The woman who is unmarried, and the virgin, is concerned about the things of the Lord, that she may be holy both in body and spirit; but one who is married is concerned about the things of the world, how she may please her husband. This I say for your own benefit; not to put a restraint upon you, but to promote what is appropriate and *to secure* undistracted devotion to the Lord (1 Corinthians 7:32-35).

Paul is not a misogynist. He sees these young women, just like their male counterparts, as valuable assets who can choose whole-hearted devotion to God over family life. Just imagine how the kingdom would change if every single woman gave her free time as a gift to God. These single ladies would be the backbone of local evangelism programs, Sunday Schools, and youth groups. Further abroad they could become heads of orphanages, administrators, doctors or nurses at missions hospitals, and coordinators of charities. The army of the Lord would be stronger if they worked instead of waited.

This positive vision of singleness, not as a time of waiting or a time of fun, but a vocation in which women serve with all the gifts God has granted them is not only refreshing (compared to the cat lady scenario), but empowering. God is not asking single women to wait for a husband, but to work for His kingdom today!

Individual Questions

1. Are you single or married? If married, how many years did you live as a single adult? How does/did your viewpoint diverge from Paul's? Did/do you make good use of your time?

2. Look around your congregation. To whom are you closest? Is her life situation similar to yours? What are the positives and negatives of dividing up this way?
How could you reach out to women in a different situation?

Group Questions

1. In your congregation are single adults put to their full use?
In other words, are they shuffled to one side or do they become teachers, evangelists, organizers, and servant leaders of other sorts?

2. Are singles segregated from the rest of your congregation?
Are they in their own class or group to do activities?
What are the positives of this practice? What are the negatives?

Married

If being single is so amazing, were the Corinthians right? Should the "real" Christians just give up their marriages and devote themselves singularly to God?

Paul has much to say to this issue beginning with the question of celibacy. The Jews had an overall positive view of sex. They not only had laws related to hygiene and sexual purity, they also thought highly of married sex (Leviticus 15, Deuteronomy 22:12-30, Song of Solomon, Proverbs 5:15-19). However the Gentiles, as Paul puts it, lived in "lustful passion" (1 Thessalonians 4:5). So this Gentile church seems to have asked Paul, "How do married people live in a God-honoring way? Is sex allowed for married people?"

Paul's answer? Not allowed, required.

The husband must fulfill his duty to his wife, and likewise also the wife to her husband. The wife does not have authority over her own body, but the husband *does*; and likewise also the husband does not have authority over his own body, but the wife *does*. Stop depriving one another, except by agreement for a time, so that you may devote yourselves to prayer, and come together again so that Satan will not tempt you because of your lack of self-control (1 Corinthians 7:3-5).

The "sexless" marriage should not exist among healthy Christians. Why? Paul says one of the wonderful things marriage does is help us to resist sexual temptation. To borrow an image from Proverbs, a hungry person is far more tempted to steal than one who is satisfied (Proverbs 30:7-9). In a marriage both partners have offered the primary authority over their body to their spouse. What a lovely image of the intimacy and "one flesh" aspects of marriage. Nothing should be forbidden or embarrassing between the two of them; each of their bodies belongs exclusively to the other.[5]

With the question of sex settled, there was still a serious issue in the Corinthian marriages. Many of them seem to have been married when they became Christians. What about those marriages? When they became a new creation, were their marriages annulled?

Paul lays out two principles. One, he says, comes straight from God. "...the wife should not leave her husband (but if she does leave, she must remain unmarried, or else be reconciled to her husband), and that the husband should not divorce his wife" (1 Corinthians 7:10-11).

The second principle he identifies as his own and applies it to not only to these mixed marriages, but also to circumcision and slavery (notably it is specifically not applied to widows and singles, 1 Corinthians 7:36-40). "Each man must remain in that condition in which he was called" (1 Corinthians 7:24). Believers are called to peace in marriage as in all else. If their spouses will stay, the believers, too, must stay. If their spouses depart, the believers must let them go in peace (1 Corinthians 7:12-16).

The two principles are not easy to swallow in our modern world. They stand in direct opposition to the basic assumptions of the world around us. The principles we see played out among our friends and coworkers as well as in our school systems and the media include...

Celibacy is unhealthy at best and impossible at worst.

Nothing is more important than being satisfied and happy.

Sex is a bargaining chip.

Yet God asks from us only what He Himself possesses in abundance. His Son lived celibately, and we can, too. He created husband and wife to be perfectly faithful and constant. On the day that God revealed Himself, these two things—His faithfulness and merciful promise keeping (often translated "lovingkindness")—were defining characteristics (Exodus 34:1-9). He asks us to live in peace with our spouse, and He is the very God of peace. Reconciliation cost Him His only Son, and He offers reconciliation as the answer to our broken relationships. If the principles seem hard to bear, it is because we are called to be like our God, a difficult thing indeed.

Individual Questions

1. Have you ever been guilty of using sex as a tool? If unmarried, take some time to set boundaries that encourage purity. If married, remind yourself that sex is not a gift you withhold from your spouse but their right as the person to whom you vowed yourself.

_____

_____

_____

_____

2. Were you married or single when you became a Christian? How have your circumstances changed since then? To what promises in your life are you called to remain faithful?

Group Questions

1. Imagine that a young married lady in your congregation comes to you and confesses that it had been a year since she and her husband had sex. What kinds of underlying problems should you listen for? What resources can you tap to help her? Besides 1 Corinthians 7, where can you go in the Bible to offer guidance?

---

2. Imagine an older lady in your congregation comes to you and explains that she was thinking of leaving her husband. They have grown apart, especially since the kids left. Now she finds him tedious and the marriage unbearable. She says, "Don't you think God will understand? I only want to be happy!" What do you say? Which Scriptures can you share with her? How can you help her understand the heart of God in this matter?

Single Again

With all that in mind, we might look around our current world and sigh that God's commands are as realistic as the princess stories we began with. All around us we find relationships shattered. Divorce is rampant. Remarriage is the norm. Many of those we talk with have given up on marriage all together and are content in cohabitation. Others have given up on the opposite sex, some to be married to their homosexual partner. This brokenness is found not only in our world but in our churches.

What are we supposed to do?

1. We must reaffirm loudly and often that God loves divorced people. That is why He hates divorce.

> "This is another thing you do: you cover the altar of the LORD with tears, with weeping and with groaning, because He no longer regards the offering or accepts *it with* favor from your hand. "Yet you say, 'For what reason?' Because the LORD has been a witness between you and the wife of your youth, against whom you have dealt treacherously, though she is your companion and your wife by covenant. "But not one has done *so* who has a remnant of the Spirit. And what did *that* one *do* while he was seeking a godly offspring? Take heed then to your spirit, and let no one deal treacherously against the wife of your youth. "For I hate divorce," says the LORD, the God of Israel, "and him who covers his garment with wrong," says the LORD of hosts. "So take heed to your spirit, that you do not deal treacherously" (Malachi 2:13-16).

Breaking apart the "two become one flesh" is devastating. Malachi warns them that divorce (in his day and perhaps in ours) is an issue of social justice. When aging men cast off the wives of their youth, God declares that their worship will go unheeded. In a challenging metaphor, Malachi says God hates "him who covers his garment with wrong" or in another translation "covers his garment with violence" (Malachi 2:16, NASB, ESV). Upgrading to a newer model (male or female) is an act of betrayal equivalent to the kind of violence that would leave a person splattered in blood. Even our modern "no-fault" divorces leave children, finances, health, and homes mangled in their wake. God hates divorce in the same way that He hates other things that hurt His children.

2. In the New Testament people did not come to God with lives already pure, holy, or righteous. We remember that as a point of doctrine and then promptly forget it in evangelism. Paul's readers included a Christian who was sleeping with his step (we hope) mom and people who had been a part of all kinds of messy sexual relationships including homosexual, pre-marital, and adulterous ones (1 Corinthians 5:1-5 and 6:9-11). As we talked about in "Evangelism: Calling the Unchurched to Christ," the lost are lost in sin, and there is no hope of advancing the kingdom if we start

117

by mentally disqualifying those who are divorced, homosexual, sexually fluid, or living with a partner.

3. We have to work to prevent sexual sin in every aspect of life. Young people must be encouraged to purity. Singles need to understand God's positive plan for their lives. Married women must be nurtured and supported especially by older women who are commanded to teach young wives to love their husbands (Titus 2:3-5). And marriages in trouble need every resource that the church can provide including counselors, babysitters, elders, and mentors. Our teaching about sexual sin must emphasize both the positive role sex plays in married life and its destructive power outside of God's parameters.

4. We have to be honest about remarriage. The issues surrounding remarriage are tricky. When 1 Corinthians 7 is compared with Matthew 5:31-32 and Matthew 19:3-9 not to mention with the more distant contexts of Deuteronomy 24:1-4 and Malachi 2, even the most dedicated Bible students may be left uncertain about how to deal with complex situations. This is not the chapter for "what ifs." Yet I would be remiss if I didn't slow down a moment and urge anyone who is divorced and considering going back to dating to examine these passages carefully, consider their conscience and their circumstances, consult their elders, and then base all actions on God's wisdom, not their own.

5. We have to stop being thoughtless and unkind. The Christian bubble can be a cookie-cutter place. We say careless things like, "Behind every good kid is a great mom" or "Your spouse is your greatest blessing." Neither of these is true. There are single dads raising godly kids, and there are great blessings outside of marriage. Saying otherwise is unnecessarily and unkindly exclusive. We are also thoughtless when we stick to the small group of people in our same circumstance (for example, married with kids in public elementary school). Although we may have much to share with them, singles, single parents, empty-nesters, and widows are an integral part of our church family and can be easily isolated.

Individual Questions

1. How has divorce been a part of your life? What have the effects been?
   Think about things like children, economics, and mental, spiritual, and emotional health. Can you see the mercy of God working now to heal the damage?

_____

_____

_____

2. Have you ever been guilty of looking at someone's sexual sin and assuming they wouldn't be interested in the gospel? Look around your circle of friends, family, and co-workers and pray for someone who is practicing sexual sin. Look for ways this week to reach out to them.

_____

_____

_____

_____

Group Questions

1. Is your congregation accepting of people whose pasts are messy? How many single parents or divorced people attend there? What would make the congregation more welcoming?

_____

_____

_____

2. Read Malachi 2 as a class. Describe what the author is seeing in his society and God's reaction to it. What does God want out of marriage? What is happening to the women? To the children? What is the result for the men? In what ways is Malachi's society similar to our own?

_____

_____

_____

_____

Princesses

Remember the childhood dream of being a princess? You know the one. You wake up one day to discover that all your mundane life has been a lie, and you are, in fact, royalty, being swept away in a pumpkin to marry a prince.

And on the one hand, it's true. We are daughters of the King. Each and every saint is a child of God. Every princess is a co-heir with her elder Brother.

Yet the Father welcomes us to be productive servants in His kingdom. There is no room for pampered and helpless girls; He needs warriors, teachers, and nurturers. His single daughters are free to devote all of their time to pleasing Him. His married daughters offer back to Him fulfillment of His original plan for a holy family, echoing Eve the first helpmeet and mother. And to all His daughters who because of death, divorce, or sin have lives that don't follow the pattern, He offers a fresh start.

He is father to the fatherless and protector of the widows (Psalms 68:5). He welcomes every kind of sinner (both the sexual sinner and the self-righteous) to repentance and reconciliation. There is no one left out, no one without work to do. Every princess is a part of His body at work in the world. ∾

Endnote

5   If you are struggling with a Christian spouse who is practicing sin such as pornography or spousal abuse, I urge you to carefully follow Jesus' instructions in Matthew 18:15-18. Christian wives have the right and responsibility to seek aid in dealing with sin for which their spouse will not repent.

CHAPTER TWELVE

RELATIONSHIPS
The Young, the Aging, and Those In-Between

Our culture declares that men and women are the same. Physiology, life experience, and even boards on Pinterest (How many men do you imagine have a board titled "My Future Wedding"?) indicate differently. In a subtlety lost entirely on the modern world, God declares that men and women are quite different, yet in His eyes, they are entirely equal (Titus 2:1-8, 1 Timothy 2:8-15, Galatians 3:25-29).

One of those differences is the feminine characteristic of being nurturers. We tend to others. We tend flowers, homes, our aging relatives, our tired husbands, and our beautiful children. We are educators, life-givers, and the protectors of the world's most helpless creatures. I don't mean that there aren't awesome dads, wonderful sons, and male caregivers in the world. There are. But tending is in our DNA.

All that desire to teach, protect, and nurture comes straight from the heart of God. If we are "mother hens," it's because our Father was first. If we are called to the faithful care of the helpless, it's in imitation of the tender care of our Lord. We are not only what He made us, we are becoming more of what He is.

Under His Wings

When I was a kid, my dad was ahead of the curve on urban farming. He had a backyard full of chickens long before chickens were cool. I remember them with all the affection of a city girl. None. Yet I still smile when I think of the time he had brooders.

I loved those fluffy yellow chicks. I would have happily smushed them against me. But their mom was having none of it. She viewed me with beady-eyed suspicion and before I could get close enough to capture all that fluffy fun, she had them tucked back under her wings.

Although I was a relatively harmless threat, hawks, foxes, and other predators were not. It's this image of the hen protectively tucking her chicks away safe from any danger that the Old Testament writers call up to describe God's relationship with His people.

The first hint of this metaphor, my Hebrew-literate friends tell me, is the verb that is used to describe what the Spirit does in Genesis 1: He brooded over the waters (Genesis 1:2). Switching from the protective care of creation to the protective care of a single young woman, the next use of the metaphor is Boaz's blessing to the hardworking Ruth. As a widow without the shelter of male in-laws, she needed protection. However, Boaz reminds us that Ruth did not run to the security of her own family, countrymen, and gods. She was faithful to her husband's mother and her husband's God.

> All that you have done for your mother-in-law after the death of your husband has
> been fully reported to me, and how you left your father and your mother and the
> land of your birth, and came to a people that you did not previously know. "May
> the LORD reward your work, and your wages be full from the LORD, the God of
> Israel, under whose wings you have come to seek refuge (Ruth 2:11-12).

The psalmists pick up this image of a terrified chick finding shelter and safety and expand on it. Under God's wings His people hide finding safety, a permanent home, and the faithful help they desperately need (Psalm 17:8, 57:1, 61:4, 63:7, 91:1-4).

Not only is God richly pictured as a hen spreading her wings over her chicks, but as a nursing mother. In Isaiah 49 God declares He intends to comfort His people, and they answer that He has instead forgotten them. To which the Lord replies,

> Can a woman forget her nursing child
> And have no compassion on the son of her womb?
> Even these may forget, but I will not forget you.
> Behold, I have inscribed you on the palms of My hands;
> Your walls are continually before Me (Isaiah 49:15-16).

Nursing mothers come with a natural timer. If they miss feeding the baby, their bodies will remind them in all kinds of unpleasant ways (pain, urgency, soaked shirts) that the baby needs to eat. Nursing mothers literally cannot forget their babies. But even if we pointed out the scores of heartless women who have abandoned mewling infants to death, God declares He does not forget.

God is the first gardener, the first parent, and the ultimate Creator. He is our Father, not our mother, yet everything to do with being a nurturer and a caregiver originated with Him.

Individual Questions

1. What is your relationship like with your mom? Your mother-in-law? Did you have a strong mother (mother-figure) who protected and cared for you? If not, have you found a sister in your congregation who loves you this way?

2. In your personal life, who can you nurture? Do you have children of your own, foster kids, in your Sunday School class, kids in the youth group who look up to you? Are there elderly people in your life who count on you as their faithful help? Read Psalm 134. Pray this prayer of blessing over some of those you nurture.

Group Question

Look up the following Scriptures. Think carefully about what the writer is finding under God's wing (joy, a home, safety, etc). How can we, as nurturers, provide these things? Think practically about situations and attitudes that allow us to imitate God.

GOD PROVIDES...	AS A CAREGIVER I CAN...
Psalm 17:8	
Psalm 57:1	

Psalm 61:4 _____   _____

_____   _____

_____   _____

Psalm 63:7 _____   _____

_____   _____

_____   _____

Psalm 91:1-4 _____   _____

_____   _____

_____   _____

Isaiah 49:15-16 _____   _____

_____   _____

_____   _____

Living Faith

We know that awesome moms are faithful (think 3:00 a.m. feedings) and protective ("Mama Bear" is a cliche for a reason). However, the Bible has examples of something else amazing about mothers: They are spiritual warriors. God's Word encompasses mothers who prayed fervently for their children (1 Samuel 1), mothers who sought out healing/exorcism on behalf of their children (Mark 7:24-30), mothers who saved their children's lives (2 Kings 4), and mothers who transferred their faith to their children.

Take Lois and Eunice for an example. We know them from their connection with their son/grandson, Timothy. Eunice, his mother, was a Jew married to a Greek. She became a Christian when Timothy was a young man. She and her mother, Lois, invested enormously in passing their faith on to Timothy (Acts 16:1-3, 2 Timothy 1:1-5, 3:14-17).

You, however, continue in the things you have learned and become convinced of, knowing from whom you have learned *them*, and that from childhood you have known the sacred writings which are able to give you the wisdom that leads to salvation through faith which is in Christ Jesus (2 Timothy 3:14-15).

How can today's mothers and grandmothers pass their faith along to the next generation? Is there a clue here?

First, Lois and Eunice had sincere faith. In any home where a woman of sincere faith lives, it won't be a secret. She will fill that home with her kindness, her prayers, her gentleness, her grace, and her hope. The fruit of the Spirit evident in her life will be evident in her home. Why? It's because hospitality, faithfulness in marriage, good works, and the care of children are both hard to miss and the basic duties of the women of God (1 Timothy 5:9-16). Timothy learned these practical expressions of godliness at their knees.

Second, Lois and Eunice made a point from childhood on to teach him the "sacred writings." The phrasing makes it plain that even before Eunice became a believer, she taught Timothy the Law and the Prophets. Though her education must have been limited and Timothy's access to the resources of the synagogue restricted because he wasn't circumcised, she managed anyway. If Eunice could teach Timothy, we have no excuse. We have Bibles, Sunday School, children's ministries, and hosts of books. We have Bible stories on CD and churches full of people eager to help us. Mothers can make learning the Word a priority for their children.

Mothers are judged on a million minor issues. Imagine if we made every decision right. Whether they were nursed or bottle-fed, when and if they received vaccinations, how they were carried, where they slept, where and how they were educated, which extra-curricular activities they pursued and how intensely. What if we were the perfect parents and yet somehow we neglected to cultivate their spirits, neglected to teach them the sacred writings and pass on our living faith, then what have we gained in exchange for their souls (Mark 8:36-37)?

Individual Questions

1. Think about how you came to believe. Who was passing along their faith? What did they do? What habits of Bible learning were demonstrated for you? How were you taught the sacred writings? Did this happen in childhood or as an adult?

2. Take a close look at your own living faith. Is it something you want to pass on to others? When you imagine your children or your students in the future, are they kinder, more

patient, or more holy than you are today? What do you need to do to become the person you want them to be?

_____

_____

_____

_____

Group Questions

1. There is a modern proverb, "God has no grandchildren." In other words no one will be saved outside of their own relationship with God. Yet Lois and Eunice are given credit by Paul for Timothy's faith. Can you reconcile the two ideas? How do we encourage children who are raised by godly parents to make their faith their own?

_____

_____

_____

_____

2. Think creatively. In today's busy world what would it take to raise a child who was "taught the sacred writings?" Please begin with the assumption that Mom works outside the home and her children are in public school.

_____

_____

_____

_____

The Aging

As caregivers, women bookend life. They are the primary caregivers of little ones: mothers in their youth and grandmothers in their age. They are also the primary caregivers of the elderly: daughters, nieces, daughters-in-law, and granddaughters who bring food, prepare pill bottles, coordinate with doctors, and sit by bedsides.

Understanding the care of the elderly begins with the fifth of the ten commandments. "Honor your father and your mother, that your days may be prolonged in the land which the

LORD your God gives you" (Exodus 20:12). Deuteronomy's version of this commandment includes not the corporate promise of holding the land but the personal promise of long life, "that your days may be prolonged" (Deuteronomy 5:16). This is what Paul has in mind in Ephesians 6.

> Children, obey your parents in the Lord, for this is right. HONOR YOUR FATHER AND MOTHER (which is the first commandment with a promise), SO THAT IT MAY BE WELL WITH YOU, AND THAT YOU MAY LIVE LONG ON THE EARTH (Ephesians 6:1-3).

These paired commands to "honor" and "obey" are established in detail throughout the old covenant. For example, the honor due a parent was extended to include honoring the elderly. "'You shall rise up before the gray headed and honor the aged, and you shall revere your God; I am the LORD" (Leviticus 19:32). Cursing a parent was lumped together with other heinous capital crimes such as giving children in sacrifice to the idol Molech and bestiality (Exodus 21:15-17, Leviticus 20:1-16 especially v9). Wisdom and morality included caring for aging relatives, listening to their wise advice, and offering them no disrespect (Proverbs 1:8-9, 15:20, 16:30, 20:20, 30:11).

These principles may seem as old-fashioned and counter-cultural to us as the ones we examined about marriage. They tempt us to excuse ourselves. For instance, "That's just their culture; America is more progressive than that." Or "Fine, honor YOUR parents, but you don't know what my parents were like."

Jesus examined the best excuse of all.

> You are experts at setting aside the commandment of God in order to keep your tradition. For Moses said, 'HONOR YOUR FATHER AND YOUR MOTHER'; and, 'HE WHO SPEAKS EVIL OF FATHER OR MOTHER, IS TO BE PUT TO DEATH'; but you say, 'If a man says to *his* father or *his* mother, whatever I have that would help you is Corban (that is to say, given to *God*),' you no longer permit him to do anything for *his* father or *his* mother; *thus* invalidating the word of God by your tradition which you have handed down; and you do many things such as that (Mark 7:9-13).

At first glance we seem to have conflicting principles. Jesus did insist following Him must come above our love or responsibility to our parents (Luke 14:26). However, we don't have here a person who is diligently trying to choose between two truths (love God and love your parents). We have a person who is using God as an excuse to escape the commandment to care for their parents.

So practically speaking how should individual saints and their congregations care for the elderly? The answer to this question is complex. However, two applications for individuals are given to us directly. Believing men must provide for their families (including the elderly), and believing women must see to the needs of their family's widows (1 Timothy 5:8,16).

The assemblies of God's people have always had responsibilities as well. Both the Old and New Testaments illustrate care for the community's widows. The tithe of Moses's law included a provision for widows (Deuteronomy 26:12-15, 14:28-29). In the early church in Jerusalem, disciples were distributing daily food to the widows among them (Acts 6: 1-7). Years later Paul wrote to Timothy with detailed instructions on how to organize and maintain the care of worthy widows without family (1 Timothy 5:3-16).

The care for the aging that is absolutely required of Christian women fits in perfectly with our overall nature as nurturers. We stand as the faithful helpers of the elderly, their protection in times of trouble, and a place of safety far from the disregard and disrespect that are rampant in the world.

Individual Questions

1. Read 1 Timothy 5:3-16. What are the characteristics of a widow worthy of the church's support? Which of these best describes you? Where do you fall short?

\
\
\
\

2. What is your relationship like with your parents and grandparents (or your husband's parents and grandparents)? Are you building a relationship now based on honor and respect? What resources are you prepared to dedicate to their care?

\
\
\
\

Group Questions

1. Read the following scenarios and discuss how to apply the principles from this section.

   A. Jackie has a full-time job and three kids in school. Her widowed aunt is having foot surgery next week. She called and asked Jackie if she could stay at their ground level home instead of going to the rehab facility (Her aunt lives in a second-floor apartment with no elevator). Imagining moving her into their three-bedroom home for the next six weeks is totally overwhelming. What should Jackie do?

   _____

   _____

   _____

   _____

   B. Margaret has never gotten along with her mother-in-law. She has always seemed bossy and overbearing. After her father-in-law's death, her husband began making noises about moving to Tennessee to be closer to her. Margaret dreads the thought. Today her boss mentioned in passing there is an opportunity to transfer to a new facility in her mother-in-law's hometown. Is it wrong for Margaret to keep this news to herself?

   _____

   _____

   _____

   _____

Reading Better

Earlier in the chapter we made the briefest mention of Ruth. The book is best known either as an example of God's work as our Redeemer or as a beautiful biblical love story. Although neither thought is wrong, there is another powerful lens through which we may view the story. Ruth was blessed because she was a caregiver.

The story begins with Ruth taking responsibility for her dead husband's mother. Even when urged to return to her family, she traveled to a new country, worked tirelessly in the fields, and supported the pair of them faithfully. The story ends with a genealogy linking Ruth and Naomi with the royal family of David (Ruth 4:16-22).

Although the text does not speak explicitly of her care of her young son, she obviously passed her faith down to him (Ruth 1:16, 2:11-12). In the morally bankrupt world of the judges, this is the only explanation that makes sense of how David was the true spiritual son of his great-grandparents (Ruth 4:16-22). She stands as a marvelous example of a faithful helper of the aging and a giver of faith to the young.

God, the life-giver, the nurturer, and the true redeemer, yearns for us to imitate Him.

He is pleased by our aid of the young and old, the most helpless members of any society. They are His powerful concern, their aid the very definition of pure religion (James 1:27). He longs to gather them under His great wings. And God longs for us, His daughters, to reflect His concern for them back into the world! ∽

CHAPTER THIRTEEN

NEW CREATURES
Stripping Off the Past

When my daughters were small, recitation was a part of our daily schedule. One of the passages we memorized was Romans 12:1-2.

> Therefore I urge you, brethren, by the mercies of God, to present your bodies a living and holy sacrifice, acceptable to God, *which is* your spiritual service of worship. And do not be conformed to this world, but be transformed by the renewing of your mind, so that you may prove what the will of God is, that which is good and acceptable and perfect (Romans 12:1-2).

We learned these words because I hoped to define for them what walking with God meant. Back then my younger daughter was small enough to find words like *transform* and *conform* hard to say, let alone understand. So we spent a long time talking about butterflies and Jell-o®.

Jell-o® conforms to its mold. Whatever its shape, the composition is unchanged. I can take the same bowl full of cooling green liquid and make stars, building blocks, or a carrot salad. Although the shapes are endless, they are all still just wiggling masses of gelatin.

Butterflies, on the other hand, transform. They go from crawling to flying. Leaf-eating machines become migrating pollinators. If a butterfly tried to become a caterpillar again, crumpled wings and slow starvation would be the sad result. A caterpillar isn't conformed to a new shape but transformed into a new life form!

Christians are like butterflies, totally transformed into the beauty and grace of our Maker. Ready to fly!

Dirty Clothes-Take 'em Off!
In one of the most disgusting episodes of my life (second only to the smashed banana escapade, *shudder*) our toilet once overflowed. Don't imagine that this is the "Oops,

someone hadn't gone in a day or two" kind of overflow. No. This was the "There's a clog in the sewage pipe somewhere underneath our first-floor apartment and every time anyone in the seven-story building flushes, the liquid is coming out of our toilet onto the floor" kind.

When we discovered the problem, our living room was already ankle deep in other people's waste water. Of course, we took emergency measures. We rolled up our pants, begged a friend to bring an extra mop, called the landlord, and sent someone to ask our neighbors to STOP FLUSHING.

Hours later, with the help of our friend with the extra mop, we had dried, then bleached every surface the water had touched. Exhausted we wanted to just drop where we stood but didn't dare sit down since every inch of our clothes had been splashed with sewage. After we dipped our noxious feet into the bleach, we went straight to the shower.

Can you imagine if we got out of the shower and put those clothes back on?

That's the image that Paul uses to talk about Christians putting the past behind them.

Do this, knowing the time, that it is already the hour for you to awaken from sleep; for now salvation is nearer to us than when we believed. The night is almost gone, and the day is near. Therefore let us lay aside the deeds of darkness and put on the armor of light. Let us behave properly as in the day, not in carousing and drunkenness, not in sexual promiscuity and sensuality, not in strife and jealousy. But put on the Lord Jesus Christ, and make no provision for the flesh in regard to *its* lusts (Romans 13:11-14).

Just like we stripped off the nasty, sewage-infested clothes, showered, and put on clean gear, Paul calls on us to strip off sin whether relational, sensual, or emotional and put on the armor of light. This theme is a familiar one (we learned about the armor of light in Chapter 10), but his urgency is imposing.

"The night is almost gone," Paul says, "the day is near." He is picking up a message that has been ringing out since the days of the prophets (Ezekiel 30, Obadiah, Joel 1:14-20, 3:9-17, Zephaniah 1:7-18). Whether five years, five hundred years or five thousand years later, the day of the Lord will come. For those enrobed in sin, it will be judgment and terror and for those who have "put on the Lord Jesus Christ" and His armor of light it will be glory. For all, the day is at hand. There is no time to wait. We cannot linger in our sin-stained garments, we must bathe and change. There's an appointment for which we dare not appear unprepared.

In Colossians, Paul returns to the question of putting off our old self with a new emphasis.

Therefore consider the members of your earthly body as dead to immorality, impurity, passion, evil desire, and greed, which amounts to idolatry. For it is because of these things that the wrath of God will come upon the sons of disobedience, and in them you also once walked, when you were living in them. But now you also, put them all aside: anger, wrath, malice, slander, *and* abusive speech from your mouth (Colossians 3:5-8).

Now instead of picturing stripping off dirty clothes, Paul imagines us taking off our dead and decaying bodies. That is exactly what he says baptism accomplishes; it "crucifies" our earthly bodies and buries them. That dead self delighted in all kinds of things that we are now ashamed of, things that incur the wrath of God, things that horrify us now (Romans 6:21). Going back to that life would be like crawling inside a corpse and trying to walk around pretending everything is okay (Romans 6:1-14).

Individual Questions

1. Are you ever tempted to view some past sin with nostalgia? Do you look back on a cozy gossip session, an illicit relationship, or the release of losing your temper, and wish for those old days? How does God view that old self and its sin?

2. The prophets and the writers of the New Testament epistles often used the words *near* or *at hand* to talk about what God is doing. Read the following passages, determine who is addressed, and surmise what the result will be.

   A. Zephaniah 1 _____

   B. Joel 3:9-17 _____

C. Mark 1:14-15 _____

_____

_____

D. 2 Peter 3 _____

_____

_____

Group Questions

1. Although we frequently study Romans 6 with baptism in mind, we don't often consider Paul's idea about Christians being dead to sin. Read this, and then trace Paul's thoughts on the death of the old self.

_____

_____

_____

_____

2. The day when God reveals Himself in power is "near" in the Bible. Is it always "near" from a human perspective? In light of the Scriptures above, is this nearness good news for everyone? What is our responsibility then (Romans 13:11-14)?

_____

_____

_____

_____

A New Creature

This metaphor of removing our old clothes or killing our old self expresses an amazing truth: Baptism washes our old sin and self away. When we came up dripping wet were we perfectly holy, the image of Jesus, righteous in behavior as well as in fact? Sadly, no. We need another metaphor, new creation, to understand this aspect of the truth.

Once long ago Adam was created in the likeness of God Almighty, a son in the image of his Father. But when he sinned, he died. Something in that amazing creation, both of Adam and the world, was broken (Romans 8:18-25). Redeeming that brokenness cost God His only Son.

Redemption is a two-legged journey. Though we continue to live in our old physical bodies and struggle with our old sin, every one of us who has "bought in" to the death of Jesus is now a new creature. Each saint has received a further pledge; he will be resurrected in the fullness of that new creation—a powerful, glorious, imperishable, eternal body (2 Corinthians 5:16-19, 2 Corinthians 1:22, 1 Corinthians 15:42-52).

As new creatures, we desperately need the renewed minds described in Ephesians 4:17-24 and Colossians 3:5-11. Our old self had a darkened mind and a hard, calloused heart. The new man needs a replacement of truth for lies, righteousness and holiness for callous wickedness, and light for darkness. Thus God offers to revive us, to return us to our original creation by recreating us in His own image.

How this renewal occurs is at the heart of a mysterious matter brought up in 2 Corinthians.

Therefore having such a hope, we use great boldness in *our* speech, and *are* not like Moses, *who* used to put a veil over his face so that the sons of Israel would not look intently at the end of what was fading away. But their minds were hardened; for until this very day at the reading of the old covenant the same veil remains unlifted, because it is removed in Christ. But to this day whenever Moses is read, a veil lies over their heart; but whenever a person turns to the Lord, the veil is taken away. Now the Lord is the Spirit, and where the Spirit of the Lord is, *there* is liberty. But we all, with unveiled face, beholding as in a mirror the glory of the Lord, are being transformed into the same image from glory to glory, just as from the Lord, the Spirit (2 Corinthians 3:12-18).

Paul assumes his readers are familiar with Exodus 19, 20, and 34. The escaping Israelites went to the foot of the Mount Sinai, and God prepared to speak to them. They were told to stay off the mountain and consecrate themselves. Although at the beginning God's people agreed to do whatever He said, after the mountain started shaking and blowing smoke, they were so terrified at having been in the presence of God that they begged Moses to stand as their intercessor. They didn't want to have to experience that terrible intimacy with Him again. Moses soon came to find out, talking to God face-to-face has strange side effects. It makes you glow. Even Aaron was afraid to come near the shining new Moses.

So he had to wear a veil (Exodus 34:29-35).

Paul parallels this Israelite desire to avoid direct contact with God (or even the person intimate with Him) with their unwillingness to read the old covenant in any way that makes the truth about Jesus Christ plain. Although they were already the chosen people of God, they didn't want Him to come near on the mountain or on the cross. Beautifully, Paul continues tweaking the metaphor. Just like Moses removed his veil and stood in the presence of God, we, too, are unveiled. We see the Lord, and instead of starting to glow with glory, we are changed. Day-by-day and again and again, we gaze at our Father and are continuously transformed into His likeness.

This process is facilitated by intimacy with God. This is not the work of a single day, as if our baptism were the entire journey instead of the first step. Rather as we pray, read the Word, and walk in the Spirit, our minds once so useless and dark, are enlightened. The righteousness attributed to us because we died with Christ and were raised to a new life, becomes slowly obvious in our behavior, thoughts, and feelings. Like a caterpillar becoming a butterfly, the change taking place will not be entirely complete until we receive our new bodies. But praise the Lord, we are "being transformed into the same image from glory to glory, just as from the Lord, the Spirit" (2 Corinthians 3:18).

Individual Questions

1. Can you describe the character of God? Use the following Scriptures to jump start your thinking: 2 Peter 3:9, Luke 11:9-13, Exodus 34:1-9 and 1 John 1:5-10.

_____

_____

_____

_____

2. Think back to your own life before you became a Christian. How was your mind calloused, hardened, and darkened? In what ways was the change to new creation instantaneous? In what ways has it been a process?

_____

_____

_____

_____

Group Questions

1. Consider the words you used to describe the character of God. How can we imitate those characteristics in our lives? For example, God is compassionate (See Jesus' example in Matthew 9:35-38 and Matthew 14:13-14). How can we be increasingly filled with compassion?

_____

_____

_____

_____

2. In the middle of the discussion on Moses's veil, there is this interesting sentence: "Now the Lord is the Spirit, and where the Spirit of the Lord is, *there* is liberty" (2 Corinthians 3:18). What is the point of the sentence in context? What is the application of this idea to our Christian lives?

_____

_____

_____

_____

Lasting Change

We are the children of God, renewed in our minds, renewed in truth and made a new creation. There are no longer barriers separating us from our brothers (Colossians 9-1). A cloud of cheering witnesses, who want to see us finish strong, surround us (Hebrews 12:1). We are transformed leaving behind us all the reek of sin and death. What might be keeping us from growing toward our Father's perfection (Matthew 5:48)?

What might be holding us back?

We might have sin lingering in our lives that should have been sloughed off (Hebrews 12:1).

We might have a person who is teaching/telling us lies that are keeping us from reaching our victory (Galatians 5:7-9).

We might not be longing for the Word that has the power to reveal who we really are. We might not have the meek attitude we need to receive that Word (James 1:21-25), and we might not have the wisdom to be doers instead of just hearers of that Word (Matthew 5).

This is the powerful challenge with which this book began: Read the Word differently. Throw off the veil, take a look into Scripture, and commit to obey. With that in mind, let's look back at the issues we have faced in this book.

Hospitality	When we receive others, strangers, saints, and teachers, we receive our Savior.
Evangelism	The church is responsible to call the world to come to Jesus.
Generosity	The Lord has given us every gift we have received and giving back to Him is simple gratitude.
Encouragement	We are anchored in Christ Jesus and call others to take courage from Him and His example.
Prayer	It is the way we develop a closer relationship with God and how we join Him in the work He is doing in the world.
Relationship	We are to be faithful the way God is faithful. Regardless of our life circumstances, we are to be caregivers the way God cares for people in every stage of life.

It is easy to feel convicted when we first read something. As I worked through each chapter, I was moved by what I was learning in the Word of God. Yet as the book comes to a close, I have to ask myself, *Have I made meaningful, lasting changes?*

Individual Questions

1. Please look at each topic, and write down what lesson you took away and one change you made. How long did you continue with your change?

	LESSON	CHANGE
Hospitality	_____	_____
	_____	_____
	_____	_____
Evangelism	_____	_____
	_____	_____
	_____	_____

Generosity _____   _____

_____   _____

_____   _____

Encouragement _____   _____

_____   _____

_____   _____

Prayer _____   _____

_____   _____

_____   _____

Relationship_____   _____

_____   _____

_____   _____

2. Do you need to revise those commitments? Do they need renewed, adjusted to be more challenging, or adapted to be more appropriate to your circumstances?

_____

_____

_____

_____

Group Questions

1. Which of the topics we've covered was most convicting to you? How have you changed? Discuss those changes with your sisters.

_____

_____

_____

_____

2. If you were going to add a topic, what would it be? Could you extend this study by each preparing a lesson and questions on the topics you chose?

_____

_____

_____

_____

Reading Better

This book began with a simple idea. We have to read the Word with a heart to obey it, not so that we can make a list of "things to do" and "things to avoid doing," but so that we can grow closer to God. I pray that as you've read, studied, discussed these issues with your sisters, confessed your sins, and prayed together, you've been transformed. We are God's children, a new creation, transformed by the renewing of our minds into the image of our Savior! May you go into the world, carrying the good news of that transformation to everyone you see so that the kingdom may grow and God may be glorified. ∾

BRIEF BIOGRAPHY

I grew up in the Asbury and South Knoxville churches of Christ in Knoxville, Tennessee. I was blessed to have parents and grandparents who did everything they could to nurture me in faith. My grandfather and my father were/are both elders in these congregations. I attended Harding University and graduated with a double major in Psychology and Vocational Ministry and a minor in Koine Greek. While there, I met my husband Kevin Smith, and we married.

Soon after we left college my husband and I both took secular jobs, bought a house, and settled into helping at the South Knoxville congregation as much as we could. I taught ladies' Bible class both in the community and at church.

In 2006 after much soul searching we (Kevin, our daughter Jael, and I) moved overseas. We taught English at the university level and quietly served as missionaries. The South Knoxville congregation served as our primary sponsoring church. During those years I did evangelism with our seekers, taught English classes based on the Bible, and taught and counseled our Christian ladies. While we were overseas, I also started writing a blog under the pseudonym, "Helene." You can find it at *maid-servantsofchrist.blogspot.com*.

In 2014 our now family of four (Kevin, Jael, Allie and I) moved back to the United States, and Kevin took a job with the Rock Springs church of Christ. Here I do evangelism with our seekers, teach the preschool Bible class, work with the girls in our youth group, take the youth group places (youth rallies, Bible Bowl, etc), and teach the Ladies Bible class.

Any writing I do, including the manuscript I am submitting, is born out of years of hands-on evangelism and teaching. In other words, I hope that any chapter I write is like any lesson I teach: Bible-based, simple, practical, and convicting.